HABITS
FOR
SUCCESS

Praise for *Habits for Success*

"*I am happy to endorse G. Brian Benson and his excellent book, Habits for Success. My father, the late Stephen R. Covey, often said that most people innately know how they should be living their lives, but unfortunately 'common sense is not always common practice.' This superb book by G. Brian Benson reveals many common sense habits that may not be so commonly practiced today. These habits are wise, proactive principles that if practiced, will greatly enhance the lives of the readers. An excellent work!*"

—Sean Covey, *New York Times* bestselling author of *The 7 Habits of Highly Effective Teens*

"*A brilliant practical informative book, which is easy to read and digest, yet has a great level of depth and wisdom to it. It is a genius tool, which can be of benefit at any stage of our life, and a great reminder for us to build practical positive habits, which will effectively create the change, we are seeking. I particularly love the 'Moments Of Clarity' as I find that reflecting upon our own journey at regular intervals is a way to build a strong foundation and to enable us to make a more positive change within our self first, which then transpires in to our life as a whole.*"

—Jolene Trister, editor of *Raw Real Being* magazine

"*G. Brian Benson's Habits for Success is the perfect blueprint to help manifest a life of progress, purpose, and fulfillment. I highly recommend anyone wanting to grow, gain self-awareness, and thrive to read his words carefully. Benson has a novel way of looking at life and expresses it in a unique and life-affirming way. There is a lot of gold within these pages. This book is a winner!*"

—Michael "Smidi" Smith, writer, producer, artist, Emmy winner, Clio winner, six-time Telly winner, with 14 million records sold worldwide

"G. Brian Benson's Habits for Success *rises above the sea of vapid self-improvement books with refreshing advice for everyone in search of change. Following his approach means you might move from pinning pretty pictures on a wish board to actually embracing your life in real time passion, and no path is devalued. This is not a compendium of formulaic bromides but advice from the heart of a man that makes confronting fear look like he was saying 'Good morning' with the tip of his hat to a stranger; he knows it's there, he just chooses not to hang out with it."*

—Mark S. Husson, founder of 12listen and 12radio.com, author of *LoveScopes: What Astrology Knows about You and the Ones You Love*

"G. Brian Benson *is a creative, conscious, and heart-centered man who isn't afraid to lead by example to help others. His book radiates vulnerability, authenticity and inspiration."*

—Prince EA, viral spoken word artist and futurist

"Brian's *keen ability to listen to his heart and to follow his intuition has laid the blueprint for all of his successful projects and has served as an example for others to follow. In the modern world, where the challenges seem to keep building up and the answers to those challenges often seem farther and farther away, his guidelines for helping everyone develop their own ability to listen and follow their inner wisdom is truly a potent and powerful way to find the guidance we all need."*

—Mark Allen, six-time Hawaiian IRONMAN World Champion and author of *Fit Soul, Fit Body: 9 Keys to a Healthier, Happier You*

"Brian's *genuine nature and happiness is what makes him an outstanding example of what it means to be a man with heart. He's an authentic writer who is full of creative ideas that he isn't afraid to see to fruition. Brian's messages are simple, rewarding and attainable!"*

—Kristine Carlson, bestselling author of the book series *Don't Sweat the Small Stuff*

"Brian's *new book* Habits for Success *is a home run! The insight he shares and the tools he provides are the perfect mix of motivation, inspiration, and wisdom, which will lead you to your own personal version of success and fulfillment."*

—Steve Decker, former Major League baseball player and current San Francisco Giants Special Assistant

"Habits for Success is a practical guide to changing your life. As a clinical social worker that works with many hearts, these simple principles are just the medicine one needs to become their very best."

—Lisa Solterbeck, LCSW, CHt, author of *Journey Back to Balance: An Intentional Path*

"Brian is one of the most creative people I know. He is a true seeker of knowledge and truth. He meets everything with an unfettered curiosity and does not shy away from the harder conversations. I love his ability to use his own journey and life's lessons as a beacon of light, hope and possibility!"

—Suzanne Hanna, creator of The Wilderness Walk and founder of Global Healing Collective

"G. Brian Benson's new book Habits for Success is an absolute guide to life mastery. In his book, he reminds us to "begin to stretch yourself out of your daily routine." This is what most of us avoid doing at all costs, yet it is the key to massive success in life.

If you feel short on time, and you don't think you can get through another self-help book, that's where Brian shines in his ability to take extremely important messages and condense them into easy to read, short chapters that anyone, regardless of how little time you think you might have, can benefit from. Don't think about grabbing this book, just do it."

—David Essel, MS, #1 bestselling author, counselor, life coach, and international speaker

"Habits for Success is a great book which will help you identify who you are and what you want in life. G. Brian Benson serves as your authentic guide to assist you in finding and living your true passion. Once you say yes to yourself as Brian tells us to do, you will find magic in your journey. Reading this book is time well spent."

—Brian K Wright, host of *Success Profiles* Radio, publisher of *Success Profiles* magazine

"Habits for Success by G. Brian Benson is truly an inspiring read in so many ways and at so many levels. Brian has shared so sincerely and openly his journey in a wonderful holistic way with great insights in learning and understanding the power of your own intuition and how to apply it to your everyday activities.

This book is like a healthy balanced diet plan to keep you in check with your wellness and prosperity. I like the way how five little things helped change Brian's life and how incredibly well written it is to change millions of other lives around the world.

As Business Owner/Coach, President with World Global Network and as an Ambassador in the Direct Sales and Network Marketing Industry with Business for home, I will be strongly be recommending it to my whole organization."

—Ghazala Jabeen, president of World Global Network

"Habits for Success speaks directly to the heart delivering practical, inspirational, and simple methods that powerfully, yet gently invite you to embrace your most authentic self. G. Brian Benson continues to lead the charge that owning and being your truest self is the key to living a successful life!"

—Jamie Dawn, author of Evolutionary Revolutionary : Compassionate Rebellion for Conscious Change!

"Success doesn't come without hard work, determination, and persistence. In my forty years of broadcasting, I've come across many books about people, both famous and obscure, who have realized their life's goals.

G. Brian Benson's new book outlines, in simple and basic terms, how to build a model for success. Habits for Success allows the reader to map out a strategy, use tools to achieve excellence, shows how to handle setbacks and disappointments, and how to build on self-confidence and self-worth. I know you will enjoy this book, and I believe you will take away many vital and memorable examples in how to build on ambition and achievement. I highly recommend it!"

—Roy Firestone, ESPN

G. Brian Benson's Habits for Success *is an engaging and inspiring guidebook to creating a foundation for living one's life authentically by creating life-changing habits. I particularly love what Brian says about not being afraid to fail, and how failure can lead us to profound lessons, new life skills, and a fresh path for giving our unique gifts to the world in ways we may not have imagined.*

> —Chuck Wild, Emmy-nominated composer with 15 bestselling albums under the Liquid Mind artist name

"*There are ways to success and happiness revealed only to those willing to do the work. In this book, Brian shares proven strategies well known by all that reach greatness in life. Straight from the heart, Brian has mined the gold for you. From his Ironman will, his poetic soul, and his Hollywood experience, Brian shows the world the infinite possibilities these enlightened ideas can create in life. What a gift: thank you Brian!*"

> —Cindy Heath, energy healer and author of *Real Beautiful: The Secret Energy of the Mind, Body, and Spirit*

"Habits for Success: *Inspired Ideas to Help You Soar is a true keeper. I have focused on this topic for decades through my radio interviews and this is one of the clearest, simplest and effective success books I have read! As an entrepreneur who took many risks to follow my dream, I not only relate to Brian's success habits, I use them in my daily life, and they are lifesavers. These habits are easy to understand but it takes discipline, belief in self, and tenacity to stay with them but when you do, the results are amazing! I have known Brian for years and have seen his growth and success. This is not a book of platitudes. Brian lives them every day and he is living proof their success! Pick up this book. It will short cut your path to success and add to your joy, happiness and sense of peace.*"

> —Patricia Raskin, *The Patricia Raskin Positive Living Show*, award-winning radio producer and broadcaster, author, speaker

"Habits for Success *was carefully crafted and easy to follow and understand even with the intricate layers of depth and wisdom. This book can propel you on to great success! Two big thumbs up!*"

> —Lacy Weston, World Champion natural bodybuilder, author of *Transform Your Reality* and owner of one of Southern California's longest-running fitness studios

"Habits for Success is a comprehensive collection of actions and mindset principles to help us not only achieve what we want, but to feel self-fulfilled in the process. As an entrepreneur, it's easy to become so wrapped up in growing the business that life gets thrown out of balance. So, for me, it was a good reminder to take a step back often and course correct before that imbalance gets out of control. I really enjoyed reading this book! It can become your first step to live the life you're meant to live."

—Cloris Kylie, MBA, influencer marketing specialist and author of the book *Beyond Influencer Marketing*

"Habits for Success has it all. Author G. Brian Benson offers an informative, inspiring, and unique look at growth, self-awareness, and success. I highly recommend this book to anyone who is interested in becoming a better version of themselves."

—Susyn Reeve, author of *Heart Healing: The Power of Forgiveness to Heal a Broken Heart*

"I love working with high achievers because high achievers are high believers. And that's why I was honored to serve as G. Brian Benson's public speaking coach, just after he made a life-altering decision to walk away from the security of the lucrative family business and blaze his own trail as an author, actor and an inspirational voice for his generation.

Every nugget of wisdom that you will read in this book was learned and earned through Brian's rigorous commitment to practicing a few simple disciplines—everyday! Brian has moved beyond belief to knowing. And he knows that Habits for Success work because he embodies them every day. Now it's your turn!"

—Kevin Kitrell Ross, author, activist, Award-Winning Speaker, Master Life Coach, Spiritual Teacher

"When you're stumbling around in a dark dungeon, and you don't know which way is out, you hope someone will turn on a light so you can find the exit door. It's even better when that someone is funny, nonjudgmental, and knows which way to go after you escape. That's what G. Brian Benson does in his book, Habits for Success. With humor, kindness, and clarity, he turns on the lights and helps you find your way out into a better you. How cool is that? Thank you, Brian."

—Dr. Carol Francis, clinical psychologist and author of *Paths to Recovery After Abuse and Trauma* and *Own your Peace: KISS Method for Inner Peaceful Living*

ALSO BY G. BRIAN BENSON

Lucy and Chester's Amazing Adventures!

Steve the Alien

Finding Your Voice

Brian's List: 26½ Easy to Use ideas on How to Live a Fun, Balanced, Healthy Life!

HABITS
FOR
SUCCESS

INSPIRED IDEAS TO
HELP YOU SOAR

Create Your Foundation of Happiness, Balance, and Fulfillment

G. Brian Benson

Mango Publishing

CORAL GABLES

Cover & Layout Design: Jermaine Lau

Author Photo: Jenny Felimi Photography

For permission requests, please contact the publisher at:
Mango Publishing Group
2850 Douglas Road, 3rd Floor
Coral Gables, FL 33134 USA
info@mango.bz

For special orders, quantity sales, course adoptions and corporate sales, please email the publisher at sales@mango.bz. For trade and wholesale sales, please contact Ingram Publisher Services at customer.service@ingramcontent.com or +1.800.509.4887.

Habits for Success: Inspired Ideas to Help You Soar

Library of Congress Cataloging
ISBN: (p) 978-1-63353-866-5 (e) 978-1-63353-867-2
Library of Congress Control Number: 2018957580
BISAC category code: PSY022060
PSYCHOLOGY / Psychopathology / Anxieties & Phobias

Printed in the United States of America

To my entire family:

Thank you for your ongoing support and love.
You have mine always.

Table of Contents

hab·it
hab-it

noun: **habit**

1. an acquired behavior pattern regularly followed until it
   has become almost involuntary.
2. a particular practice, custom, or usage.
   "This can develop into a good habit."

Introduction

As I was making the thirty-minute drive to South Pasadena High School, site of my impending TEDx talk, I turned on the radio in search of some musical inspiration that would both pump me up and quell my nerves. I knew this day would come when I decided to share my story on the TEDx stage. But now that it was here, it felt surreal. Preparing for it had become part of my daily life—I carefully chose every word, rehearsed it alone in my apartment, in front of my acting class, while out hiking, and in front of any friend who would listen. And, more often than not, I danced in that confident space where I could deliver this speech just as I had been successfully practicing it countless times. I was excited and ready. Not just in an "I got this" way—but also in an "I have arrived, and no more playing small" kind of way.

Sure, I had my moments of doubt, but each time they crept in I gently pushed them away, finding that soulful center that had always created a safe haven and guided me intuitively forward. For me, that burning desire to follow my inner voice—and hunch—often turned out to be a beautiful and unexpected experience. So, when I turned on that radio, I was taken aback to hear these exact lyrics: "There's no place to hide, but I don't think I'm scared."

Those words cut me to the core. That was going to be me in only an hour! I would be on the TEDx stage in front of a large, live audience with cameras rolling, and had no place to hide. But was I scared?

The lyrics hit me hard, and raw emotion came pouring through me. Instead of fear, I felt validation hitting me square between the eyes, saying, "You are ready, you are prepared, and you deserve this moment." I recalled all the things I had worked so hard to do prior, just to be able to stand on that stage: speech classes, Toastmasters, co-hosting my own radio show, acting and improv work, creating my own workshop, and writing books. It had been a challenging march, fluctuating between courage and doubt, bordering on self-flagellation, to gain enough confidence to share my story in front of others.

Although each step strengthened my foundation, that foundation was about to be tested. Would I be rock steady as I let down my shields and insecurities in front of that packed theater? I thought so. My tears were a tangible reaction to the lyrics; my intuitive inner knowing supported the tears. I was ready. I wanted this test. I knew I could and would welcome the audience sharing in my vulnerability.

When we share our truths, pains, and imperfections, we shine light on our true essence. It brings us closer together as a community because that is what I believe we all truly desire in our lives: authenticity and sharing. Offering and receiving authenticity creates joy. When we reveal ourselves, we stand unencumbered in truth: there is no place to hide.

Living authentically and openly this way is freeing: I have never felt more free than when I walked off that TEDx talk stage after sharing my journey with (potentially) the world. I will continue to stand on that stage, albeit a figurative one, as I move forward with more adventure, learning, and sharing. I want you to stand up and shine on your own proverbial stage as well. There is quite a beautiful view to be had when we look out from our heart. And I know I'm not scared. And I don't think you are either.

CHAPTER 1

My Journey

jour·ney

noun: journey

1. a traveling from one place to another, usually taking a rather long time; trip.
2. a distance, course, or area traveled.
   "His **journey** *was long, but was rewarded with learning and self-awareness."*

Ten years ago I was running my family business. I had been running this business, which was a successful golf center, for eleven years. We had a driving range, a nine-hole golf course, and a retail golf store in Salem, Oregon, called Cottonwood Lakes. But I was really unhappy.

I know a lot of people would give their "left arm" to have that job, but I didn't feel like I was being my true authentic self and that bothered me. Up to that point in my life I had accomplished some really nice things. I rode my bicycle across the United States, finished over fifty triathlons (including four Ironman races), had a wonderful son, and was running a profitable business; so a part of me felt like I had a good understanding of personal success and what that meant and felt like. But I wasn't feeling that way *at* my job or in my life anymore. I felt like I had this giant gift inside of me that wanted to come out, but I didn't know what it was; I just knew that it needed to be released. So, with a slightly confused heart, I left the golf center and my family's business. I had no idea what I was going to do with my life after leaving, but I trusted my decision.

Now, getting to the place of actually leaving the business was much harder than I just made it out to be. This was a job that had permeated through my being ever since I was a seventh-grader driving a little tractor with a makeshift wire cage on it to pick up the golf balls. I would effortlessly drive around lost in thought on warm summer evenings, smelling fresh-cut grass and listening to the "thwack" of club hitting ball, and compulsively picking up every single one of them come the end of the night so the customers could do it all over again the next day. I had grown up with that job; it taught me responsibility and gave me purpose. It provided me a consistent workplace throughout high school and during college while home on summer break. It also made me "cool" and gave me instant credibility amongst my peers, not to mention a handy place to take a date. But most importantly, I had grown up playing golf: it was a sport that provided many happy memories for me as a child and a vital tool that helped my father and I bond, and that made it one of the reasons why it was hard for me to tell him I didn't want to do it anymore as an adult.

In my heart, I think I always knew that I wasn't going to be working at the golf center for the rest of my life. I felt an intuitive tug pulling at me early on during my eleven-year tenure of running the facility. It was the same tug that I bravely followed into triathlon racing during college, but this tug wasn't quite strong enough or, more likely, I didn't have the courage to listen to it at that time to actually leave. But now it pulsed stronger than ever and wouldn't allow me to stay complacent in something that wasn't my true calling. That didn't make the initial conversation about wanting to leave the business with my father any easier. At first I felt that I was letting him down. My thinking was that he had provided me with this great opportunity to run and co-own a business that most people would happily say yes to. And I knew that he had secretly hoped that I would make it my own someday.

When I finally did gather the courage to have the chat, the conversation went much better than I could have ever imagined. I think much of the anxiety stemmed from my own fears of letting him down. He told me that he sensed I wasn't enjoying it as much as I had been at the start of my eleven-year run and that he certainly didn't want me to do anything that my heart wasn't into or be someone that I wasn't. He also told me that he just wanted me to be happy. I felt very fortunate that my father understood my feelings and was able to let some of his own fears be tabled.

He also shared something with me that totally caught me off guard. He told me that if he could have done it all over he would have become a golf club professional instead of an independent insurance agent, because he loved to teach and help others with their golf game. (He had a very long and successful career as an independent insurance agent while we operated the golf center on the side.) He sensed that he understood my need to find my true calling, whatever it may be, while I still had time to explore and find myself. All of the guilt I was carrying in regard to my departure had been placed there firmly by myself and by my own expectations of potentially letting him down after having this great opportunity presented to me, which I would soon be leaving.

I think many of us have been taught by society and our loved ones (as they were taught as well) that happiness and fulfillment come from fitting into a certain societal mold. Be wary of being seduced into prematurely accepting some role that doesn't have much to do with your nature or values. The familiar model is to head to college, get a job, get married and have kids. Unfortunately, that expectation sometimes clashes with information we are receiving from our heart and intuition. At least that was the case for me. As a result, I was initially caught in a situation of feeling like I was letting my dad down by following my heart.

Looking back on my experience at the golf center, with ten years of perspective under my belt, I have no regrets. I learned a great deal about myself, people in general, and business—I wouldn't change a thing. But most importantly, it helped shape me into who I am today. It gave me the tools and knowledge, both tangible and emotional, that I carry forward. I am very proud of the fact that I followed my heart and listened to my intuition, and I consider myself lucky that I had the courage to walk away from a secure yet unauthentic situation.

I feel like I am living my authentic life now. I have found happiness and fulfillment in writing, speaking, producing, and acting. I am accomplishing things that I never would have thought or dreamed possible. It wasn't until I left my job that I really began to see how alive I could feel, simply by being myself and following my heart.

When I stepped away, I didn't really know who I was or what my future held. What I did know was that I sure wanted to find out. I had to step away from something that I didn't love in hopes of finding something that I did. There began the process of building a new, more stable foundation for the rest of my life.

> *We are all just walking each other home.*
> **—Ram Dass**

I love this quote, always have, and always will. It cuts right to the heart of the matter. We are all here basically going through the same experiences, dealing with primarily the same problems, and trying to do our best to survive and thrive in a sometimes-difficult world. We all have so much in common. And at the deepest core of our existence we all want the same beautiful thing, to love and be loved. Why do we make it so hard for ourselves? Fear and painful experiences just to name a few. Why can't the process of "walking each other home" be easier, if we all basically want the same thing? I think it can be.

As I share my journey, I want you to have your own journey. It's never been my intention to tell anyone what to do. I want to share my experience of how I am "doing life" in hopes that you can gain more personal awareness so that you can "do your life" in as fulfilling and as enjoyable a way as possible. I want to share with you how I created habits by living authentically that strengthened my foundation. I want you to be inspired to want to live your life to the fullest.

There comes a time in all of our lives when it becomes more painful for us to stay mired in our old habits than to step outside our comfort zone and risk the unknown as we journey toward finding our true voice. Your true voice is the language of authentic fulfillment, joy, and happiness. While speaking your true voice, creativity flows, fears subside, and peace of mind prevails. I truly want everyone to find his or her true voice.

It took me over forty years to begin to find and speak my true voice. I had to overcome my own internal beast. The beast that tells us that we are not enough. It is the ultimate internal battle of overcoming feelings of unworthiness. Things looked successful on the outside, but I certainly can assure you that I struggled on the inside. I did the work to find out who I really was and to become what I have always wanted to be: a more authentic version of myself.

It's ok to have fear and be scared. According to author Steven Pressfield, "Fear is a good thing. Fear is an indicator of what we have to do. The more certain we can be of the importance of the enterprise, the stronger degree of fear or strength of resistance you will have." Interesting, huh? This really hit home with me. When I began my journey after leaving the family business, I had a lot of fear and resistance as I began that process. But I knew the importance of what I was undertaking in regard to my own self-growth process and the intuitive pull I was feeling. I had to step into that.

Interpersonal work is not easy. It's a private journey that only you and you alone can take. It takes courage; it takes a belief in yourself that may not be fully developed or present as you begin the process. It's a trust walk upon a darkened path into the unknown. But it is so worth it. You truly will be the butterfly coming out of its cocoon. Unload your baggage and find true self-acceptance. It is the greatest gift you can give yourself and others. Walk with me, and let's journey together.

CHAPTER 2

Your Foundation

foun·da·tion

noun: **foundation**

1. the lowest load-bearing part of a building, typically below ground level.
2. the basis or groundwork of anything.
   "Her **foundation** *was extremely strong."*

When we think of a foundation, we typically envision a building of some sort, perhaps a house or a skyscraper. When a house is built, the strength of its foundation is key. This is the anchor that supports the entire structure, preventing it from blowing away and holding it strong and steady despite potentially changing climates and conditions. You wouldn't think of building a house or a skyscraper without putting that essential first layer into place, would you? Well, the same is true for us. If we want to live authentically and be the best versions of ourselves and accomplish our goals and live out our dreams, the first thing we need to do is build a strong foundation. It may seem like a simple part of the overall construction process, but getting the foundation right is incredibly important. Our "house" sits on top of it! And since the main purpose of the foundation is to hold the structure above it and keep it upright, a well-built foundation keeps the building standing while the forces of nature potentially wreak havoc. It keeps its occupants safe during calamities such as strong winds and earthquakes. Well, the same thing applies to us as well. If we don't properly build our foundation, we open ourselves up to all types of forces boldly wreaking havoc on us. Forces like judgment, low self-esteem, fear, untruths, inaction, jealousy, resistance, apathy, and imbalance, just to name a few. Our foundation should be built with care because it determines how strong and firm our "house" will stand. And how strong our "house" will stand determines how fulfilling, authentic, and successful our lives will be.

Take, for example, all of those creative folks who enter sand castle building competitions. They make building their incredible creations look so easy. If only that was so. I once read where an award-winning castle builder explained her process. She mentioned that interested onlookers often complimented her on the creative details of her work, but what those onlookers don't realize is that her most diligent efforts were spent on the building of a solid foundation first. Generally the first two hours of her process were spent analyzing the sand content, digging until the most ideal grains are found, then saturating the sand and applying pressure to compact it into a solid formation. And then, and only then, can she get to work on the impressive detailing of her sand creation. But without those initial steps and a solid foundation, the entire structure could collapse. When we have a solid foundation under us, truly anything is possible.

I would like to share some of my favorite ideas, tools, and habits I developed that have helped me build and maintain a stable and healthy foundation in my life. These activities have been instrumental in helping me find my way, keep me on my path, learn and grow, and to see the world differently. Some may already be a part of your life, some may be new; either way, let them sink into your being and see what comes up for you.

As you implement these changes into your life, be patient. Some things will be subtle and feel effortless; others will require work on your part to rewire some of the habits that have anchored themselves into your life. Never fear, you can do it! You will find that having a strong foundation gives you energy, drive, and a sense of purpose.

As I have walked my path these last ten years, I have paid attention to what worked, didn't work, what brought me joy and what caused me pain and problems. Much of what I have experienced or gone through is laid out for you to gain from. I want you to operate from an incredibly sound foundation. And I know that these ideas are tried-and-true.

There is no rhyme, reason, or level of importance to the order that these gems are presented; however, they are all potentially life changing. May they help build your foundation of success like they helped me build mine.

CHAPTER 3

Strive for Balance

bal·ance

noun: balance

1. a mental steadiness or emotional stability; habit of calm behavior, judgment, etc.
2. a state of equilibrium or equipoise; equal distribution of weight, amount, etc.

"The man strived to live a life of **balance.***"*

There is a quote that I like that says, "We are here to teach what it is that we need to learn ourselves." I want to share with you how that quote played a part in my own self-growth process. During the course of leaving my family business, I was stuck in a kind of limbo for a year. In my heart I was ready to hit the road and begin my new life, but I had to stay around and continue to operate it while we went through the process of finding a buyer because of the decision to sell. I began to feel really out of balance and I didn't like that feeling. I wanted to figure out why I was feeling out of balance. The answer was pretty simple. I was in a job that no longer fulfilled me and I felt that I wasn't growing anymore. Well I knew that there wasn't much I could do about this until we sold the business, so I had to make the best of the situation. I then decided to try to figure out how to bring some balance into my life. What I did was simple. I just sat down and wrote five things on a piece of paper that I felt might help keep me balanced and centered and then stuck it in my wallet. From that day forward every time I began to feel out of balance or out of center, I would refer to my list and make sure that I was following its suggestions.

One— Make sure I was drinking enough water daily.

Two— Make sure that I was getting some daily exercise.

Three— Make sure that I was getting enough sleep each night.

Four— Allow myself some daily alone time so that I could re-energize my system.

Five— Allow some time each day to be creative. At that time in my life, it was from playing the guitar.

This helped me out so much that I intuitively thought, "Hey, why don't I expand the list and make it into a book to help others in the same way that I helped myself?" It was a great experience. I learned a lot in the process, I met some amazing people at workshops, and I know that the book helped many others in the same way that I was able to help myself! "We are here to teach what it is that we need to learn ourselves" played a part in the creation of my first book, *Brian's List!: 26½ Easy to Use Ideas on How to Live a Fun, Balanced, Healthy Life!* As I worked on and learned how to stay in balance and build a strong foundation for myself, my path led me to help others do the same thing.

What is balance? According to the dictionary it is a state of equilibrium; mental steadiness or emotional stability; a habit of calm behavior and judgment. I agree. For me, balance is when everything is in alignment and I feel calm and centered. It is a time when I can make decisions proactively and not reactively. How do I know when I am out of balance? Usually when I start to feel overwhelmed and have difficulty making progress on goals. This is definitely my cue and a huge reminder to take a step back and begin to implement some tried-and-true methods to get me back in balance.

It is critical to have balance in our lives for many different reasons, most importantly because it gives us a solid foundation from which to operate. Without a solid foundation, it is very difficult to stay focused and move forward toward our goals and dreams. Without balance it can also be a struggle to listen to our intuition and guidance, which is crucial as we learn how to follow our hearts and move forward on our path. Another reason it is important to have balance in our everyday life is because balance makes it possible to be fully alive and to live by making choices in the moment. When we are in balance we have the energy, attention, and space in our lives to seize new opportunities. When we are in balance we can more easily recognize potential pitfalls without falling headlong into them.

Why Is It Important to Have Balance In Our Lives?

- We have more energy—Because we have eliminated many of the things that aren't really important to us that have a tendency to weigh us down.

- Things flow smoother for us—Living in balance makes it possible to be fully alive and to live by making choices in the moment. We become proactive, not reactive. We make decisions because we want to, not because we are forced to.

- We are able to be our true selves—We can focus on what it is we want to do, not what we might have to do.

- We have a solid foundation to operate from—Without a solid foundation, it is very difficult to stay focused and move forward toward your goals and dreams as well as just your everyday common tasks.

- Our intuition becomes clearer/louder—The greatest thing about being in balance, I feel, is that we are able to live from our heart. And when we live from our heart, we are better able to listen to our intuition and guidance and act on it. Author Sonia Choquette has a great quote: "When we disconnect from our heart, we disconnect from our life source." That's why it is so important to lead a balanced life.

What Are Some Things That You Are Currently Doing That Keep You In Balance?

1. _____

2. _____

3. _____

4. _____

5. _____

Why is it so hard to maintain balance in our everyday lives? One reason is because balance can act like a moving target. From day to day, our own individual point of balance can change depending on how much energy we have available and where our focus is. Let me give you an example: have you ever seen a juggler who keeps throwing another ball into the air? What do you think is eventually going to happen? He will eventually end up dropping some of his balls, right? What do you think is going to happen if you keep adding tasks, events, and items to your daily grind? Eventually some of these tasks won't be finished or successful, will they? Just like the juggler with too many balls in the air, the more things we have going on in our life, the more difficult it is to keep everything going without dropping the ball. As the pace of our lives accelerates, so does our need to stay in balance.

Why Is It Hard to Stay In Balance?

- Balance acts as a moving target. From day to day our own point of balance can change depending on how much energy we have available and where our focus is. Every day is different for us.

- Our lives have become busier. The more we have going on in our life, the harder it is to stay in balance.

- We don't know ourselves well enough. According to author Don Miguel Ruiz "awareness is the first step toward personal freedom." Staying in balance and harmony really comes down to self-awareness.

- We might be involved in something that doesn't suit us. If we are doing something that we don't want to do or isn't right for us, we are definitely going to be swimming upstream. I learned this first hand when I was running my family's business.

What Are Some Things That You Are Currently Doing That Knock You Out of Balance?

1. _____
2. _____
3. _____
4. _____
5. _____

How can you come to have balance in your everyday life? The first step is to identify that you are out of balance. Common signs of being out of balance are feelings of being overwhelmed, continual stress, poor health, and difficulty in making progress on goals. If any of these examples fit you, you are probably feeling stress due to being out of balance. What to do? Start out by taking a deep, cleansing breath, identify the reasons, and then begin to focus on making things simpler.

How Do We Stay In Balance?

- Identify that you are out of balance—Some common signs are feelings of overwhelm, continual stress, poor health, and difficulty in making progress on goals.

- Get to know yourself better; pay attention to your feelings—Paying attention to your feelings is the best way to get to know yourself. As you become more self-aware you can learn about what keeps you in balance and throws you out of balance, as well as begin to implement that knowledge and create better habits and truly live a balanced life.

If you find yourself feeling intense, balance it with some lightness.

If you find yourself working too much, balance it with some play.

If you find yourself giving too much, balance it with some receiving.

The list is endless...there is always a counter for something we are doing too much of.

- Focus on making things simpler—Simplifying life is the easiest way to find and maintain balance. When you have time to rest, to think about what has happened prior and what's next, it is natural to come back to center. And when you are at center, you can make proactive choices on how you want to live your life.

What Are Some Ways You Could Simplify Your Life?

There will be times when you are out of balance. It happens to all of us. But, as you become more aware of what makes you tick, those moments of being unbalanced will become shorter because you will have the knowledge and tools to turn things around as you get to know yourself better. That is the key!

It's no coincidence that my first book was about establishing life balance. I feel grateful to have learned how to become more self-aware and to realize the importance of staying in balance at such a crucial time in my life. It helped me to build and solidify my foundation as I began my new journey. My self-growth process began to expand after paying attention to and learning about the different facets of balance and I became hungry to learn about other ideas and ways to thrive.

CHAPTER 4

Trust Your Intuitive Nature

in·tu·i·tion

noun: intuition

1. a direct perception of truth, fact, etc.; independent of any reasoning process.
2. a keen and quick insight.
   *"She learned to trust her **intuitive** nature."*

Intuition is the language of the Soul. When we listen to our intuition we are fed information from our higher self. Its communication is most clear when our mind is quiet. This information is Divine. It can lead you to your true purpose as well as fulfillment and peace of mind.

Listening to and trusting your intuition works in all facets of your life. You might receive a positive or negative feeling about a person you just met or whether or not to take a particular job you are offered. You might receive an "all systems go!" intuitive hunch in regard to a project that has presented itself. Or you might receive a "cautionary" feeling while dealing with someone you are dating. Make sure that these hunches are not being manufactured by your mind or out of fear. There is definitely a difference when it comes from our intuition. Our mind has a fantastic way of trying to hijack the proceedings and make determinations about what we should do for all sorts of reasons; usually not the right ones. Remember your mind is being run by your ego and the ego always has a way of stepping into our business.

Intuition can be communicated to us in many different ways.

Feelings of Restlessness—This was definitely the case for me as I began to feel it was time to leave my family business. I started to feel unsettled, unhappy, and that it was time for a change. When you are feeling like it's a time for a change, it's important to pay attention even if your feelings don't make logical sense. They didn't for me. I had a well-paying and secure situation, yet it was time for me to branch out and explore new challenges and learn from new experiences. Your soul knows when it's the right time to move forward and will help guide you to do so.

You Have a Sense of Peace and Confidence Even When Your Decision Doesn't Seem Rational—I definitely felt an incredible sense of peace and calm once I told my father that I would be leaving the business, so I can certainly relate to this form of intuitive communication. Even though I didn't know what my future held, the feeling I was receiving was an "All systems go!" When your intuition speaks to you, you will feel confidence and clarity; when your ego speaks, it will present itself as uncertainty and fear.

You May Notice a Recurrence of Thoughts or Opportunities that Keep Presenting Themselves to You—If you are getting intuitive hits or hunches about something and you aren't listening to them, they may continue showing up for you in different ways until you finally get the hint. Your brain may wander back to a particular thought, you might hear the same message in a song, or you might see a particular image pop up on television or on the Internet. Pay attention to these repeated signals. It is your intuition trying to get your attention.

Dreams and Visions—Pay attention to your dreams. They can offer tremendous guidance and a roadmap for change. The idea for my short film Guitar Man came to me in a dream one night. When I woke, I felt inspired and felt a sense of incredible duty to write down what I dreamt. Although I had never made a short film, nor even acted, very shortly thereafter I met a young filmmaker and we made my dream a reality. It was an incredible experience, which opened up many new doors for me. Visions are no different. You might have pictures or images come up for you while you are daydreaming or just going about your business. These can be nudges or guidance to try something new or move in a particular direction.

A Gut Feeling—This feeling can hit you when you meet someone, walk into a room, or possibly have an important decision to make. It can affect you in a couple of different ways. It may come to you in the form of a peaceful or excited feeling accompanied by butterflies or as a sinking, uneasy feeling that is a sign that something is off. It's important to honor and pay attention to both signals as they could be signs that you are either headed in the right direction or that you need to be very cautious and wary.

You May Become Ill—When you ignore your intuition and its repeated attempts of communication it is absolutely possible that you may create stress or bring illness into your life. Physical signs like anxiety and sickness can edge into your life because you are ignoring your intuitive signs that you need to change something.

You May Feel Inspired and Have a Sense of Knowing—You know your intuition is speaking to you when you feel excited and inspired! I can certainly relate to this. Prior to all of the projects that I brought to fruition, I felt a rush of excitement, energy, and desire to make them happen. I knew with all of my heart that I was supposed to proceed.

Honoring your feelings isn't always the easiest route to take…or the most popular. But I can tell you that it is the right route. Being honest with yourself is the most important thing you can do. And learning how to trust your intuition and allowing it to guide you in life is priceless. Trusting my intuition has been the single most important thing that I've learned on my journey, second only to learning how to truly love and accept myself.

Remember when I made mention earlier in the book about how my intuition guided me during the process of leaving my family business as well as all of the unique guidance it gave me in my journey? I wouldn't be where I am today, had I not paid attention to and trusted my intuition. Although everything didn't necessarily make sense as I was going through it, it was all perfectly orchestrated. I would follow one hunch, which led me to the next step, which would lead me to another intuitive hunch, which led me to another step, and so on and so forth until, before you knew it, my foundation became pretty darn strong and I had created a fulfilling life for myself. A life that continues to leave me excited and inspired because it was intuitive inspiration that guided me each and every step of the way to get here.

If you want to begin to listen to and trust your intuition, there are a few things that you need to be aware of. It's important that you begin to strive for balance in your life. I have found that when I am out of balance, it makes it harder for me to "hear" my intuition coming through. I also enjoy spending quite a bit of my time in quiet settings. I am not telling you to live the life of a monk in total silence, but if you keep music blasting all of the time or even the TV for that matter, it is going to drown out your ability to foster your intuition. Some people are afraid of silence or, better yet, they haven't allowed themselves the opportunity to experience it. There is nothing to be afraid of. Feel the beauty in silence and allow whatever is supposed to come up show itself. While possibly uncomfortable at first, it will be healing and you will then be able to begin to trust your intuitive nature by opening your channels to receive it. It is there for all of us to use. We just need to give it permission to show itself by creating a receptive environment.

According to author Thomas Condon, "Intuition is a lot like dreaming. We don't know how we do it, but we do it. Intuition is knowing something—but not knowing how we know it." I totally agree. In its very simplest terms, intuition is being open to and listening to your heart or guidance. Do you know that most of the information we use in our daily lives is unconscious, and that we "know" much more than we realize? That little bit of information should "wake up" everyone and make you realize that tapping into your intuition is so very important.

Why do some people trust their intuition and act on it, while others ignore the important guidance being given them? I think some of the reasons are as follows:

Haven't Been Taught How

There are many reasons why people don't utilize their gift of intuition. One of the main ones is because most people haven't been taught how to use it. Growing up, most of us were taught to feed our mind, our ego, and our thoughts, instead of our hearts. We only became comfortable with using and believing in the five senses: sight, hearing, touch, smell, and taste. It is time to add a sixth sense—intuition. As a result, many of us have found ourselves in situations that weren't very fulfilling. I can attest to that when I originally made the decision to run my family's business. In my heart, I knew it wasn't going to bring me true fulfillment.

As people become more aware of their inner guidance and the benefits of listening to it, it may still be hard for them to fully subscribe to following this guidance out of fear. Fear from breaking free of the only way of thinking and operating they have known. But you know what? It's never too late to change one's habits. Those habits we are addicted to, that never allow us to fully shine. It's time to acquire new habits that help us build a strong, balanced foundation so that we can listen to our intuition. It's never too late to trust your inner guidance and honor your feelings.

Lack of Trust

Another thing that can hold people back from listening to their intuition is lack of trust. Of course this corresponds with the fear example, but there is a difference. Some individuals may intellectually agree with the idea of listening to their intuition or heart, but haven't made the plunge because they have yet to see results. For them it is a lack of trust that is holding them back, not necessarily fear. To those individuals I say: Just go for it! What do you have to lose? Think back to the days when you were a youngster getting ready to jump off of the diving board for the first time. The water was there for your safe landing. This situation is no different. This time, you potentially have peace of mind, fulfillment, and happiness waiting to catch you.

Out of Balance

Without a solid foundation it is very difficult to stay focused and move toward our dreams and goals. While training for my Ironman races, I worked very hard at staying in balance with healthy habits. I made sure to get enough sleep, eat properly, and eliminate the things that threw me off-kilter. When we are in balance we can make proactive choices instead of reactive choices. When we are in balance, that intuitive voice is much stronger.

I know how important listening to my intuition was as I made the decision to get started in triathlons. And it was just as important for me as I embarked on my bike ride across the country. In both situations I felt like I was being guided toward both endeavors. Although at the time I might not have been able to explain what I was thinking or feeling, I did know that I liked the way it felt as I began exploring these new adventures. It felt like: "All systems go!"

Ways to Improve Your Intuition

Meditation. During meditation we are able to give our brain a rest from the busy life and schedule that most of us lead, which in turn helps us to feel more rested, balanced and centered.

Lead a healthy lifestyle. Eat better and eat less. Exercise. Proper hydration. Getting enough sleep. These are all great places to start.

Strive for life balance.

Practice maintaining an open-minded, playful, experimental, nonjudgmental attitude. Daydream, doodle, brainstorm, and write down words or phrases that come to you when problem-solving.

Work at eliminating negativity from your life.

Yoga. Yoga is wonderful for men and women for a variety of reasons. Not only will it help you build strength and flexibility, yoga is also a fantastic practice for slowing down and quieting our bodies. And when we slow down and quiet our body, our mind quiets down as well.

Rhythmic Exercises. There are many forms of rhythmic exercise that can help strengthen your intuitive abilities as well: walking, running, swimming, tai chi, and the aforementioned yoga. As your body goes on "auto-pilot" during these exercises, it allows your mind to take a rest and allows your intuition to come through.

Learning how to listen to your intuition takes some time and trust on your part. Your ego might try to interfere, but if you practice and pay attention, you will eventually learn the difference between the two. The more you listen for and trust your intuition, the more you will begin to rely on it and let it guide you. That is when life really gets interesting!

Moments of Clarity

Are you paying attention to your intuitive feelings and hunches?

Do you trust your intuitive feelings?

How do you receive its guidance?

CHAPTER 5

Step Out of Your Comfort Zone

com·fort zone

noun: **comfort zone**

1. a situation or position in which a person feels secure, comfortable, or in control.

   "Growth comes from working outside of our **comfort zones.***"*

What is a comfort zone? It seems to me anything that helps keep our anxiety in check. The comfort zone, as defined by Alan Henry, is a "behavioral space where your activities and behaviors fit a routine and pattern that minimizes stress and risk." The important words here are stress and risk. Since a comfort zone is a place to help keep our anxiety in check, I would also imagine it houses a sense of security and familiarity. So when we leave our comfort zones, we're basically taking a risk and opening ourselves up to the possibility of stress and anxiety because we aren't sure what is going to happen next.

Shilpa Chatterjee says: "Although anxiety is not exactly something we go chasing after, a little bit of it can actually be healthy. A hint of anxiousness can push us to take risks, get more done, and continually better ourselves. Healthy stress acts as a catalyst for growth, motivation and optimal performance." I wholeheartedly agree. When we step out of our comfort zone and challenge ourselves, we are provided with so many new gifts. First and foremost, I think that we become more productive. As we expand our capabilities and break through barriers, we find new, exciting possibilities in every aspect of our lives. Your creativity will increase as you have new experiences and learn and grow from them; your creative abilities will develop and broaden.

I can attest to this personally. After I left my family business and began to follow my intuition, all kinds of creative opportunities and gifts started showing up that I didn't know were inside of me. Another benefit of leaving one's comfort zone is that you will begin to have an easier time dealing with new and unexpected changes. Which in turn will make it easier to continue to push your own personal boundaries and continue the process of stepping out. Yes, please! And finally, you will achieve more. Nothing ventured, nothing gained. If you don't step out of your comfort zone, how do you expect to write that children's book that you've been thinking about or finishing that marathon you have always wanted to run? When we challenge ourselves to accomplish something difficult, new gifts will be unveiled, you will be given the strength to continue on, and unbelievable things happen.

After writing my first book back in 2009, my intuition was telling me that I would need to learn how to be more comfortable in front of people, especially if I was wanting to share and market my book. The proposition of giving a speech or talking to a group terrified me, but I honored what it was telling me and I knew what I had to do. Over the course of a couple years, I really dove in and began the process of learning how to be a more comfortable speaker and quell my anxiety. I started off by taking a couple of community college speech classes, which was then followed by joining Toastmasters for about a year. I then hired someone to co-host my own Internet radio show, I took an acting class, and I also created an "interactive workshop" that I could offer people that tied in with my book. I ended up calling it "An Introduction to Balance." I basically had my intro memorized and then I would hand out worksheets to the participants and we would discuss their answers as a group. I thought I was being really clever, because it was a way for me to speak and be in front of others without having to talk the whole time! It turned out really well.

All of these things that I did were definitely steps out of my comfort zone. I had to show up, with shaking knees and all, to meet them head on. But you know what? I not only survived, I thrived. As I continued to say yes and step forward, with newly developed habits, I was rewarded with wonderful experiences, newfound confidence, a strengthened foundation, and peace of mind that came from a soul on purpose. As my roots grew deeper, it became easier to continue to step out of my comfort zone in many different ways.

When we are being true to ourselves and moving toward authenticity, others will bear witness and want to do the same. I think that is incredibly important. It's a great way to find and share inspiration along the journey. And believe me it will be nice to have some supportive, like-minded people walking alongside you. You can share ideas, be accountability partners, and it's always a great thing to have someone to celebrate a win with!

Helpful Hints for Stepping Out of Your Comfort Zone

- It's ok to start by taking small steps. This will allow you to get comfortable with your initial discomfort of trying something new.

- I would like to see you also begin to do whatever it is you are doing on a regular basis. It will help you get more comfortable with being uncomfortable as well as help you keep up your momentum. It's important to challenge yourself continually. It will get easier, I promise. You will begin to feel more confident and alive.

- Try to reframe your fear into excitement. It's a way to view what you are doing in a positive light instead of a potential negative light. When I said yes to do my TEDx talk, I tried to focus on the exciting aspects. For example: getting to share my story with a lot of people, the positive opportunities it might lead to, and the growth that I was going to be gaining. Instead of: "What if I screw it up and thousands of people see it when the video is released?" or "What if I forget what I am supposed to say and freeze in terror?" for example. It's all about focusing on the positive versus the negative and if you can hold that space, you will be fine!

- Remember why you are stepping out of your comfort zone. When you focus on your reason, that can give you a huge boost of courage, energy and focus. Maybe you feel that you have an important message to share, like I did. Maybe you have a fear of flying, but you need to get across the country to support a family member. Remember why you are taking the risk and how much the reward means to you.

- Mix things up. Hang out in new locations. Visit a new restaurant. Wear something different. Begin to stretch yourself out of your daily routine. It's a great way to begin the process of taking bigger steps out of your comfort zone.

Great things happen when we step out of our comfort zones and follow our heart. Doors open, opportunities are presented, and knowledge and confidence are gained. "Life begins at the end of your comfort zone," according to noted author Neale Donald Walsch, and I couldn't agree more. You got this!

Moments of Clarity

When are some times that you have stepped out of your comfort zone? How did that feel?

What are some ways that you could step out of your comfort zone?

CHAPTER 6

It's OK to Fail

fail

verb: **fail**

1. to fall short of success or achievement in something expected, attempted, desired, or approved.
   "The experiment **failed** *because of poor planning."*

Go fail a few times. I am being totally serious: it will teach you so much.
It will help you build character. It will make you humble. It will teach you to dig deeper. It will make you more empathetic. It will teach you new ways to do things. And it will lead to other opportunities.

Without failure, we wouldn't become the people that we are meant to become. It is such an important part of building our foundation of success. You grow and build strength through the process of failure. While that doesn't make it any easier going through it, things do get better and you will gain clarity. Think of it as a means to an end. As you get used to the feeling of "having been there before," each new time you step out of your comfort zone, the process will get easier and your confidence will grow. That's a huge win all by itself.

What if you do fail? So what, keep trying. Just because you weren't successful in your first attempt doesn't mean you won't be successful in your second, third, or tenth attempt. Each attempt is a powerful learning experience. All successful people have had setbacks or bumps along the way to their success. The beautiful thing is that they didn't allow these setbacks to stop them from attaining their goals and dreams. English novelist John Creasey received 753 rejections slips before he went on to publish 564 books. It took Thomas Edison ten thousand attempts to perfect the light bulb. These are both amazing stories of perseverance, fortitude, and trust, of following a dream and doing everything possible to make it happen.

For some, the fear of failing keeps them from even starting. So when I say "go fail a few times," it is to get you to move past that initial hurdle. I had to really be aware of this when I started out acting. Every bad audition I had stung incredibly and even kept me from attending others, because my confidence was so low and I didn't want to keep embarrassing myself. I let it beat me up—almost to the point of throwing in the towel. But I kept on, and soon I started to occasionally book jobs. I became more relaxed at auditions and just tried to stay out of my head, to be myself, and to live in the present moment. That really helped me. You are no different. Just keep at it, whatever it is. You will learn, you will get better, and you will begin to succeed. It's ok to fail. In fact it's recommended.

A Minute of Failure

A minute of failure can lead one to grow
Or tumble and stumble to the depths far below
The decision is yours, what to do when you fall
To pack up and quit or stand firm and tall

Everyone fails; it's natural and true
It's part of the process to grow and become new
So pick yourself up and give try again
If you find yourself failing, it's a fleeting trend

Don't give in to failure or you will never be set free
It's for those who don't believe, and lack vision to truly see
Keep standing; keep standing, each time you fall down
Your true nature will emerge, your spirit unbound

—G. Brian Benson

Moments of Clarity

What was the last thing you failed at? How did that make you feel?

Did that failure keep you from trying again?

CHAPTER 7

Get Creative

cre·a·tive

adjective: **creative**
1. resulting from originality of thought, expression, etc.
2. having the quality or power of creating.
   *"The child confidently tapped into their **creative** abilities."*

Did you know that creativity is considered the highest form of intelligence? Sure, we need to have knowledge, but to keep taking steps into the unknown and to truly let our highest realms of possibility come through us we need to exercise our creative abilities. We are all creative at some level. Some folks might be able to express their creativity through painting while another expresses it playing the guitar and yet another through writing. The important thing is that we are expressing ourselves. When we create we are allowing a force greater than anything we ever thought possible to flow through us and express the Divine.

Being creative can also act as a form of meditation. I can easily get lost in the rhythm of creation. It's not surprising that there's now a big market for adult coloring books. To be able to joyfully get lost in a coloring book or while creating something original can be very grounding. It is also a wonderful way to strengthen your foundation. It doesn't matter if your painting is up to the standards of a Van Gogh or that your poem matches the brilliance of Walt Whitman. All that matters is that you are expressing yourself.

Not sure where to start? Just experiment. I certainly didn't expect to become a writer after I left my family business. But there came a point where I felt like I had something to say and I began to experiment, first with rhyming children's stories, poetry, and then self-help. You are no different. Go take a drawing course, an acting class, or a writing workshop. See what happens. Pay attention to how it makes you feel. Don't be afraid to express yourself in ways that you may never have expected. Listen to your intuition and follow the joy it brings you. I have found that I am happiest when I am being creative. It is one of the few times when I know I am doing exactly what it is I am supposed to be doing and I can get out of my head and just be at total peace.

And it is never too late to create. Georgia O'Keeffe worked steadily into her nineties, continuing her tradition of fine work. French impressionist Claude Monet painted well into his eighties, even after cataracts clouded his vision. Acclaimed architect Frank Lloyd Wright completed the design of the Guggenheim Museum in New York at age ninety-two—and Giuseppe Verdi wrote *Falstaff*, thought of as his most renowned opera, at the age of eighty-five. Get creative! You may just surprise yourself.

My friend Kimberley had been a writer her whole adult life. After her husband died, she studied occupational therapy and eventually wrote a book for children with advice about coping with grief that used both her writing and OT skills. She realized that she would need pictures to go with it. She then painted what she thought would be a good cover, to give an illustrator an idea of what she wanted. After being pleasantly surprised by what she created, she ended up painting all of the illustrations for the book! She laughed that it took her a week to write the book and two years to paint the fourteen canvases. She said the skill just grew itself. She improved so much in two years that she had to go back and repaint some of the earlier canvases, because they didn't look like the same artist.

Kimberley took her new creative skill and started teaching acrylic painting at a local craft store. Currently she is teaching art and music to kids with disabilities, using her OT skills again. She felt that her book project magically pulled her through all the steps to get to her current teaching position. And to think that she never painted or drew until she was in her fifties, when she illustrated the book. Incredible! That definitely proves the point that it is never too late to be creative.

Moments of Clarity

What are some current ways that you enjoy expressing yourself creatively?

What are some new creative outlets that you might enjoy?

CHAPTER 8

Take a Moment for Yourself

mo·ment

noun: moment
1. an indefinitely short period of time.
2. the present time or any other particular time.
   *"She loved to take a few **moments** to get centered."*

With today's world becoming busier and busier, it's no wonder people are having trouble functioning, not to mention suffering from stress-related health problems. Having technology at our fingertips makes it much more difficult to separate ourselves from work and all those people who may want to track us down. For many it feels like our "on" button is never shut off. With cell phones, email, text messages, and social media, it can feel downright overwhelming to steal a moment's respite to get centered and regain our bearings. However, doing so will allow you to replenish and feel much more in balance. Allow yourself a few minutes every day to relax and do some deep breathing. It will make all the difference and help keep you energized throughout your day. Take a short walk, sit down in a park, and eat lunch in silence. If you can't get away from your place of work, sneak out to your car and close your eyes. Take some deep breaths to regain your sense of self. You may have to get creative to create some space for yourself, but it will be well worth it.

One of my favorite things to do is take a 20-minute meditation-catnap in the afternoon when I am starting to feel tired and need a refresher. I turn on some relaxing ambient music and let it play while I sit in my favorite chair. Sometimes I even briefly fall asleep. I ALWAYS feel refreshed, centered, and ready to get back to work after I do this. It's an incredibly important habit that I have incorporated into my life, and I don't know what I would do without it. Whenever we can take some time and step back, even if just for a few minutes, new pathways open for us, our mood changes, and we can regain our sense of balance.

Moments of Clarity

What are some ways that you could take a moment for yourself?

CHAPTER 9

Be Vulnerable

vul·ner·able

adjective: **vulnerable**
1. open to moral attack, criticism, temptation, etc.
2. capable of or susceptible to being wounded or hurt.
   "Sharing his personal story left him feeling **vulnerable.***"*

To authentically open up requires vulnerability on our part. I realize being vulnerable isn't easy, but it is well worth the effort. I have struggled myself, because I too can be quite introverted, but as I continue to share and open myself up I have found an incredible freedom from the process.

And believe me, it doesn't all happen at once. It is a process. Looking back, I would share glimpses of what was really going on inside of me through a blog, a poem, or even disguised in the form of a short film. Just glimpses. It was all that I could do at the time. It was hard for me to share any more than that. The short film *Searching for Happiness,* which I wrote and acted in a few years back, is a great example. The film's message shows one man's journey to overcome his unhappiness and loneliness. He is eager to learn how to be happy but isn't sure how to do it. Without completely spoiling the end, he finds it through witnessing random acts of kindness by strangers. And throughout the film we creatively highlighted how he views these interactions to strengthen the message. I am very proud of how it turned out. I didn't realize it at the time, but I wrote *Searching for Happiness* for myself.

I had to open up and be vulnerable in sharing that experience with others because ultimately it was about me. While I didn't fully understand it at the time, I certainly do now and am thankful for the process and opportunity of being able to be vulnerable and share my journey like that. Not only did it help me strengthen my foundation, it was a very cathartic and beautiful experience that made me feel alive. I don't ever want to close that part of me off again.

There are few things more inspiring than to see another person become vulnerable and share a part of him or herself. It gives the rest of us permission to do the same.

I remember when I felt inspired over a period of time to write some poetry. It was around 2011, a few years after I had left my family business and I was really doing a lot of work on my own self-growth process. I felt these poems come out of me almost magically. I felt like I was a conduit. One of my favorites is a poem called "Light." At the time, I could sense that I was headed in the direction of wanting to be a self-help author and speaker, and these poems were a way that I could try and connect with others to let them know that they were enough and that it was ok to truly be yourself. It was my hope that these words would inspire others to see their true value and worth.

Looking back seven or eight years later, I realized that the poems I wrote and the words that came through me were once again for myself, just like the film *Searching for Happiness*. At that time I had yet to fully love and accept who I was and what I had to work with. I was still trying to convince myself that I was enough; I had yet to fully embody my self-worth. Those poems that came through me were beautiful messages sent to remind me of my worthiness and perfection. I just didn't see it at the time. I thought they were for others and *their* reminder.

I will also say that it took some courage on my part to share them when they first came out. I had not read much poetry and had certainly never expected to be writing any. I initially felt quite sheepish. I felt exposed, which is another way of saying "vulnerable." But I got over that and began to feel empowered with the words that I was able to share with others and I truly enjoyed the process of creating them, just as I enjoy the process of creating self-improvement books and children's books. All different and unique, yet they all come from a willingness to share myself from a place of vulnerability. It's worth it, my friends.

Light

Can you see your light inside you?
It shines both day and night
Leading you both near and far
Keeping your path in sight

Can you feel your light inside you?
As it courses through your veins
Inspired greatness housed within
To share for all to gain

Can you taste your light inside you?
Flavored sweet and pure
Water, land, and truthful food
Grant energy and cures

Can you hear your light inside you?
As it speaks to you in song
Guiding you to flow each day
Helping you stay strong

Can you touch your light inside you?
Compassion, joy, and heat
A tender kiss, a warm embrace
Rituals to be complete

Can you sense your light inside you?
It's spoken from within
Hunches, feelings, heartfelt signs
Giving life a whole new spin

Will you trust your light inside you?
Your gifts, your being, your core
True greatness lies in wait
To be shared, enjoyed, explored

—G. Brian Benson

Moments of Clarity

Do you allow yourself to be vulnerable?

If not, why?

How could you be more vulnerable?

CHAPTER 10

Hang In There When the Going Gets Tough

tough

adjective: **tough**

1. hard to bear or endure.

   *"She showed a lot of courage when things got **tough**."*

Dreams. We all have them. They fuel our existence, they let us ponder a brighter future, and the path to realize them fills our lives with excitement, fulfillment and growth. I want to share a story with you from an experience I had where I wasn't sure if I was going to be able to realize a dream of mine. It was back in 2006 and I was entered to race in Ironman Arizona (a 2.4 mile swim, 112 mile bike and a 26.2 mile run), which was being held in Tempe near Phoenix.

I found myself at the race start treading water with twenty-three hundred other people in Tempe Town Lake. Twenty-three hundred other people! Now I don't know if any of you have participated in or witnessed a triathlon mass swim start with twenty-three hundred people, but I can tell you one thing: it isn't pretty. To try and help you visualize what I am talking about, imagine a massive piranha feeding frenzy. It is one large mass of arms and legs flailing about, with folks getting kicked in the head and goggles getting knocked off. The first ten minutes are quite intimidating to say the least, even for an accomplished swimmer.

Being a strong swimmer I had not expected any problems, but right after the cannon went off to start the race I started having a panic attack. I began to hyperventilate, my heart raced and anxiety pulsed through my body. I was truly scared and felt an urgent need to try to get over to the side of the lake. After a terrifying couple of minutes of trying to regulate my breathing and keep my head above water, I worked sideways through a tangled mass of swimmers and reached the bank.

First thing I tried was to slow my breathing down by taking deep breaths. I began to relax slightly as I held onto the bank and removed myself from the churning rush of arms and legs, but still felt confused, scared, and anxious all at the same time. Confused as to why it had happened, and scared that I might not be able to continue and finish the race. I felt my goal slipping away.

Luckily for me, the deep breathing exercises really helped my anxiety begin to pass. After about five minutes of mindful centering, I made my way back out into the water and proceeded to complete the swim portion. For a moment though, I didn't know if I would be able to head back out and finish. It really scared me. Anxiety attacks are frightening on land, but to have one in the water was a whole other level of terror. My Ironman dream that I trained for, visualized, and made sacrifices during the previous year for almost didn't happen.

I can tell you that the feeling of triumph, relief, happiness, and fulfillment felt even sweeter when I crossed the finish line fourteen hours later, after the terrifying start to my morning. At the beginning of the day I felt like I knew how things were going to go and what my path to reach the finish line would look like, but life threw me a curveball, as it does sometimes, with the panic attack. It also turned out to be ninety-seven degrees that day, which was also quite unexpected. I had to refocus, dig deep, and allow things to unfold differently than I had originally planned. I still accomplished my goal because I held my intention, kept moving forward, and overcame the rough start. I just had to be open to taking a different route to get to the finish line.

Hang in there when things get tough. This is where your training and habits for success come in handy. I can guarantee you anyone that has ever accomplished anything has had difficult moments and experiences on his or her road to success: it's just part of the deal. It's not always easy or the way we want it to go, but it builds character, hones our intention, strengthens our foundation, and makes us stronger for the next potential roadblock. You got this!

Moments of Clarity

When was a time that you stayed in there when the going got tough?

How did that make you feel?

CHAPTER 11

Let Go of Judgment

judg·ment

noun: **judgment**

1. an act or instance of judging.
2. the forming of an opinion, estimate, notion or conclusion, as from circumstances presented to the mind.

   *"He had a tendency to **judge** others based on hearsay."*

I had the pleasure of doing one of my workshops, *An Introduction to Balance,* a few years back to a group of twenty-one teenage boys who were incarcerated at a youth correctional facility in Oregon. One of the nice things about that particular workshop is that it had a tendency to be a bit different each time because of its interactive nature and the flow of the different participants that come through. What I witnessed that day while presenting to these young men will stick with me for a very long time. I had no idea what to expect or what kind of reaction I would get from them and truthfully was nervous that there wouldn't be very much interaction. What happened totally blew me away.

Instead of having a lot of silence and looks of "why am I here" from the youth, I found many very intelligent young men who couldn't wait to speak and share their experiences, their regrets, and their dreams. Some talked of already having forgiven their peers or family members who played a part in having them incarcerated in the first place. Many talked about how they wanted to go to college and how they were going to make it happen. Some talked about wanting to raise healthy families even though it wasn't something that was modeled for them while they grew up. Others talked about forgiving themselves for the crimes that they committed so that they could move forward. A few of the boys even mentioned that they had separated themselves from their mothers or fathers, brothers or sisters, and friends to get away from their past of violence, crime, abuse, and gang interaction. I felt so honored to be in that room with them listening and sharing.

I even had one teen tell me how he wanted to eventually be a youth counselor so he could help others like himself break free of their pasts and lead healthy futures.

He told me that although he had no credits toward his high school degree when he was incarcerated, in two years he had almost completed his GED and would soon be able to start taking some college-level classes. He then went on to tell me some of the pressures he is facing to make that dream happen. Apparently a friend of his, a member of the gang he used to be a part of, was recently shot by a rival gang member. The rival gang member was caught by the police and would possibly be sent to the same facility where the teen is incarcerated. The teen has received letters from the leader of his former gang telling him he needed to avenge his friend's shooting when the rival gang member arrived. He shared with me that he was really feeling a lot of pressure internally to honor his gang's wishes. But he stayed true to his dream of helping others and getting his college degree. I can only imagine how difficult it was for him.

I left the facility after the workshop feeling blessed in so many different ways. Blessed that I had a happy and healthy childhood. Blessed that I didn't have as many obstacles to face to reach my goals and dreams as these young men do. Blessed that I had the opportunity to play a small role in helping these teens learn more about themselves and to give them an opportunity to share. And blessed that I had the humbling opportunity to learn from them and realize what a gift freedom and choice is; something that they currently don't have. And most importantly, blessed to be reminded to never, ever judge a book by its cover. A strong foundation has no room for judgment.

Moments of Clarity

Have you ever found yourself judging another person or a group of people without knowing them?

And if so, did that change if you had the opportunity to know more about them?

How did judging them make you feel?

CHAPTER 12

Boldly Say Yes

yes

noun: **yes**

1. an affirmative reply.
   *"She loved to say **yes** to challenges."*

Yes is such a simple yet powerful word. It can transform lives, move mountains, and change the world. Saying yes isn't always easy, but it's worth it. To say yes requires trust: trust in yourself, trust in the hunches that you are receiving, and trust that you can accomplish whatever you are saying yes to. More than likely it is something that you haven't had the opportunity to do before. And that involves risk. I knew that I was headed in the right direction if something felt both "scary and fun."

One of the things I am most proud of is the fact that I have continued to show up and say yes. Yes to trusting my intuition. Yes to leaving my family's business. Yes to my personal self-growth process. Yes to continually stepping out of my comfort zone, and yes to all of the projects that I felt compelled to bring to life. I have learned that saying yes sets an intention of success as well as creating a positive flow of momentum; both incredibly important as we create new habits and build our foundations for success.

The benefits of saying yes far outweigh the alternative. When you say yes, you stand to grow, gain confidence, improve your situation, create new opportunities, lead with your heart, be an inspiration for others, achieve your goals, live out your dreams, have unique experiences, reach new heights, and truly feel alive.

To say yes also means to take control of a situation. Sometimes you need to step up and just say, "I got this. I am going to do whatever it takes to put this together and make it successful." I learned that each time I took control, it got a little bit easier the next time, and the next time, and so on and so forth. Taking control of a situation builds momentum, and momentum builds confidence.

I also know that there can be times where you feel like you want to take control of a situation but aren't quite sure how. You ask yourself, "How will I make it happen?" You know what? It's ok that you aren't sure how you will make it happen initially. All that matters is that you have a goal or a dream and are committed to making it happen. Once that is established, boldly say yes and start moving forward. What does moving forward mean? It can mean any number of things. It just depends on what you need to manifest your goal. Do you need money to finance it? Go figure out how to raise it, whether it's from a part-time job or convincing others to back you. Do you need to educate yourself about a certain topic? Go take a class or talk with an expert on the subject. It's alright to ask questions and learn from those who do know. Most people are happy to help. Do you need to get hands-on to begin writing or creating? What are you waiting for? Take control, say yes, and get the process started.

In 2015, I received a phone call from a gentleman that I had briefly met while I was living in Reno, Nevada, named Ben. Ben now lived in Los Angeles and told me he was curating a TEDx event in Pasadena and felt like I might be a good addition to the roster of speakers. Would I like to do it? At that time in my life I hadn't ever really given thought to doing a TED talk, but I was certainly aware of them. I had very much enjoyed the informative and inspirational nature of the presentations that I had watched on YouTube. So when he asked if I wanted to do it, butterflies immediately filled my stomach and a million things ran through my head. When? Where? How long do I have to prepare for it? What will I talk about? Do I have what it takes? What if I screw up and thousands of people see me screw up watching it on video? Will I be able to memorize a 15-minute talk? You get the picture. I immediately went the fear route. But almost just as quickly I took a deep breath and realized that although it would be a potentially scary proposition, I also felt like it could be a fun opportunity and an incredible experience to learn and grow by. My intuition was banging the drums go for it! So I gulped and said yes, and trusted that I could do it and that everything else would fall into place. Which I am very happy to say that it did. It was a truly empowering experience for me, and I am so glad that I had the opportunity to share my talk. I learned a lot about myself and gained another level of confidence from the event. I also met a whole bunch of really kind and cool people. What more could I ask for?

As Christopher Robin once shared to Winnie the Pooh, "Promise me, you'll always remember that you're braver than you believe, stronger than you seem and smarter than you think." I couldn't agree more. Boldly say yes. It will be the best thing you ever did.

Moments of Clarity

When was the last time you boldly said yes?

What could you boldly say yes to now?

CHAPTER 13

Just Be You

you

pronoun: you

1. one, anyone; people in general.
    "You do a really great job of staying true to yourself."

I have always said, "Love yourself and everything else will fall into place." I really believe this. And from my own self-growth process and journey I have witnessed this to be true. When I could get to the point of truly being alright with who I was—and I mean *really* loving myself, warts, flaws and all—and being ok with what I had to work with, it seemed like so many previous issues I had struggled with just seemed to ease away. Relationships became easier because I was coming from a place of bringing the "real" me, not the person that I thought someone wanted me to be. I wasn't looking for someone to fill my voids anymore.

My work became more confident, authentic, and honed because I didn't have to waste a lot of time or energy hiding the real me. There is a huge weight that gets lifted off of our shoulders when we can sit comfortably in our own skin.

To "just be you" is to trust that your desires, ideas, and thoughts are enough, and that you have nothing to prove or explain to anyone because of them. My attitude changed as I began to accept myself. I found that I became more grateful and relaxed. That is definitely no accident. I wasn't looking outside of myself anymore, feeling like something was missing.

I remember feeling like I needed to be perfect and almost pious when I started writing self-help books. I really did a huge disservice to myself. I am by nature a witty, fun, and playful person. I held that part of me back, after my first books were written. I mistakenly thought that since I was writing about self-improvement topics, I needed to be a model of perfection for the readers. Which is actually the furthest thing from the truth. I attached a lot of unnecessary pressure on myself and became quite unhappy. I just needed to be me.

Society certainly isn't doing us any favors with all of the body image advertising coming at us—advertising that can make us feel less than whole and send messages that we need to buy their product to become lovable. Social media has also trained us to see only the best of others, while we unfortunately compare that with the worst of ourselves. Our self-esteem has been hijacked to only feel validation when others hit the "Like" button for us.

Please remember that you are perfect and enough just the way you are. Comparing yourself with others benefits no one. I used to compare myself to others as I started out and it would leave me feeling depressed, unworthy, and unsure of my next step. Once I realized that my set of tools, gifts, and experiences were my superpower, everything started to fall into place. I let go of worrying about what everyone else was doing and began to trust my uniqueness. I want you to trust your unique set of tools, gifts, and experiences as well. It is an imperative part of solidifying your foundation.

Be yourself to free yourself! You are amazing.

Come On Down

Come on down it's time to shine
And leave your fears at bay.
They aren't real, illusions guise
It's time you shared your say.

Come on down it's time to be
Present in life's grand flow.
Centered, balanced, trusting thought
Intuits guiding know.

Come on down it's time to share
Your gifts, your life, your core.
Sublime march unique to you
Which opens faithful door.

Come on down it's time to trust
Spirits inspired plan.
Gentle nudges of support
Firm foundation to stand.

Come on down it's time to feel
Free your heart, mind and soul.
Release the pain, taste the joy
Of playing your true role.

Come on down it's time to love
Life, yourself, your story.
You are truth, complete and whole
Birthing perfect glory.

Come on down it's time to live
It surges inside you.
Your hopes and dreams need to breathe
And shine their colored hue.

—**G. Brian Benson**

Moments of Clarity

Where are some areas of your life where you aren't being authentic with yourself?

How could you do a better job?

LIGHT BULB MOMENTS

The Self-Growth Process

We delight in the beauty of the butterfly, but rarely admit the changes it has gone through to achieve that beauty.

—Maya Angelou

Do not be embarrassed by your failures, learn from them and start again.

—Richard Branson

Transformation is an ongoing process that tends to appear ordinary, when in fact, something extraordinary is taking place.

—Suzy Ross

The first step toward change is awareness. The second step is acceptance.

—Nathaniel Branden

The great solution to all human problems is individual inner transformation.

—Vernon Howard

Yes, your transformation will be hard. Yes, you will feel frightened, messed up and knocked down. Yes, you'll want to stop. Yes, it's the best work you'll ever do.

—Robin Sharma

Growth is the great separator between those who succeed and those who do not. When I see people beginning to separate themselves from the pack, it's almost always due to personal growth.

—John C. Maxwell

It's always best to challenge yourself and go to a place out of your comfort zone.

—Eliot Sumner

Real transformation requires real honesty. If you want to move forward…get real with yourself.

—Bryant H. McGill

The key to our transformation is simply this: the better we know ourselves, the better equipped we will be to make our choices wisely.

—Greg Braden

We are what we repeatedly do. Excellence, then, is not an act but a habit.

—Will Durant

CHAPTER 14

Happily Expect the Unexpected
(There Are No Rules)

un·ex·pec·ted

adjective: **unexpected**

1. not expected; unforeseen; surprising.
   "The job offer was an **unexpected** *surprise."*

I had no intention of becoming an actor or an author. They weren't even on my radar. I originally just signed up for a beginning acting class a few years back because I thought it would be another tool to help me become a more confident speaker. But I would soon find out that it would become an important part of my self-growth and creativity process, not to mention an important part of strengthening my foundation.

Shortly after starting that first acting class, I had an idea come to me in the form of a dream one night that was about a street guitarist. When I awoke, I immediately wrote it down and tried to make some sense of it. At the time I was a closet guitar player and I had never played in front of anyone before. I ended up giving a young filmmaker I had just met named Michael Sweeney a call and asked if he wanted to hear an idea I had about a potential short film.

We met a few days later in person and he loved the idea. No more than a few weeks after that we found ourselves on the streets of Reno, Nevada, making a short film that I wrote and acted in called *Guitar Man*. I didn't really know what I was doing; I just knew that I wanted to do it. I had a vision. And with Michael's experience and help we made it happen. It was a very powerful experience for me. I felt totally alive! I had never acted before, and I certainly had never played guitar in front of anyone and there I was doing it on film. *Guitar Man* ended up getting accepted to eleven film festivals, but more importantly it opened another door for me. Someone else saw that film and gave me the lead role in a film he was producing. On that film I met a very talented and experienced actress who became a good friend and was also instrumental in helping me move to Los Angeles a few years later. Which in turn led to other projects, opportunities, and growth experiences. Acting, just like writing, found me because I simply listened to my intuition. I had no expectations. I just kept an open mind and I showed up. Once I began to realize that there were no rules and that my path didn't have to look like everyone else's, I relaxed and my whole world opened up. I now happily expect the unexpected. I want you to as well.

Moments of Clarity

Are you open to all the possibilities that are out there for you?

Or do you find yourself trying to control every aspect of your life?

CHAPTER 15

Connect with Others

con·nect

verb: **connect**

1. to establish communication between; put in communication.
2. to join, link, or fasten together; unite or bind.
   "He loved to **connect** *with like-minded people."*

In today's fast paced, instant gratification, super-size-me world, where people's lives are broken down and validated into social media "likes" and "tweets," it's very easy to forget to take a long deep breath and remember what life is really all about. It's about people. It's about people, and how much we all really have in common. We all have hopes and dreams. We all have fears. We all go through struggles and make mistakes. We all want to be heard and acknowledged. But most importantly, we all want to love and be loved.

Most of our days are spent at any number of places being surrounded by other people. It could be at school, work, gym, or the grocery store, just to name a few. But how well do we really get to know these other folks? Are we making an effort to do so? Or are we "too busy" to even notice? It also appears to me that there is a lot of negativity and judgment going on these days. What's up with that? We all have much more in common than the perceived differences that we share. That's a good thing. Life would sure be boring if we were all the same.

We all have stories. We all have unique experiences that make each and every one of us different from everyone else. But we also have a tremendous amount in common, even though our cultures and customs may be different. We all are here doing the best we can, with what we have to work with. Falling in love, raising families, wanting the best for our children, finding joy, and dealing with heartbreak and loss. I believe that when we open ourselves up to other people's stories, it has a way of making our own experiences richer and more valuable. And it also helps us realize that we are generally one and the same even if we share a different religion or way of living.

Dr. Dean Ornish said, "The need for connection and community is primal, as fundamental as the need for air, water and food." I agree, and I realize it may be a bit hard for some of you who may be on the introverted side. I understand, because I am as well. But connecting with others is a crucial piece to building a strong foundation. Once I made the effort to reach out more by connecting and chatting with strangers I met during the course of my day, it really lifted my spirits and made me feel less isolated. I always felt better after saying hello or engaging in a brief conversation while in line or in passing. It made me feel connected and part of something much greater. And if someone didn't smile back or engage in conversation that was okay too. Everyone is on his or her own journey. And at least I knew I'd made the effort.

I recently read about a British hairdresser who was giving haircuts to the homeless. He would walk the street on his days off and volunteer his time. His story really inspired me. What a powerful gift to help people, who often feel unseen and hopeless, have a sense of worth. Through a simple act of connection, he was able to let these folks know that they have value and dignity.

So the next time you interact with a cashier at the store, walk by a person asking for help on the sidewalk, or make a deposit to the clerk at your bank, give them a smile and remember that they are just like you. Through connection we live richer, more satisfying, and expansive lives.

Moments of Clarity

How can you make a difference in your life by connecting with others?

Do you find it easy to connect with others? If not, why?

CHAPTER 16

Get Away

a·way

adverb: **away**

1. aside; to another place; in another direction.
2. far; apart.

*"Any chance to get **away** was a plus in her book!"*

Are you tired, mentally blocked, and feeling like you are going through the motions? You owe it to yourself to get away. Give your brain a rest, let your cup refill, and honor yourself with some fun. Lots of ways to do it: Hop in your car and go take a day trip. Spend a couple of nights in a hotel a few hours from home and be a tourist. Take that flight to Hawaii or Europe that you have always dreamed of. Life is short, and your emotional and physical wellbeing deserve to be treated like royalty! Most importantly, when you return you will be rejuvenated and ready to get back to work. I can't tell you how many times after I got back from an extended trip or weekend getaway that my creativity, energy, and intuition just flowed for me.

Allowing myself to get away hasn't always been an easy thing for me to do though; my driven nature can keep me going, which makes it hard to slow down and give myself permission to step away. But after the realization that many of the times that I tried to push through and be productive and creative, nothing would happen, I started to honor my feelings of stepping back and giving myself a break.

I remember feeling at wits' end a few years back. Every ounce of me was screaming to get out of town for a little while and refuel. So after making a few arrangements to be gone for about ten days, I got in my car and drove through the southwest with no agenda. I ended up spending a few days in Flagstaff, Arizona, which allowed amazing day trips to the Grand Canyon, Sedona, and Jerome. The natural beauty and history of each place lifted my spirits immediately! I felt at peace. I then drove through Monument Valley on my way up to Colorado. It was quite a treat to see the gorgeous monoliths in person that I remembered from all of those classic John Wayne western movies. I then headed up into Colorado and made Durango my home base for four nights while I made day trips up into the mountains. It was a truly refreshing and exciting experience to see such a unique part of America. I just turned off my brain and went with the flow. I saw some incredibly beautiful country with a heightened perspective, met some really kind people along the way, and returned home feeling rejuvenated and feeling much gratitude. I want the same for you. You owe it to yourself. It doesn't matter if it is one day or one month; just give yourself permission to get away! Go explore and see the world with new eyes and a wondrous spirit, and come back a different person.

Moments of Clarity

When was the last time you took a trip or a got out of town?

If it was too long ago to remember, how does that make you feel?

Where would you like to go?

CHAPTER 17

Have Patience While Learning

pa·tience

noun: **patience**

1. quiet, steady perseverance; even-tempered care; diligence.
2. an ability or willingness to suppress restlessness or annoyance when confronted with delay.

   "Some say that **patience** *is a virtue."*

Self-growth isn't easy, and it can be very frustrating and sometimes even embarrassing (trust me, I know), but it's worth it. It takes patience, unconditional love, and honest communication with yourself as well as to those you are journeying with. I truly think there is no greater gift you can gift to yourself or to a loved one than to be open, honest, and willing to explore those areas where we are not whole.

Keep venturing forth; keep exploring who you are and what makes you tick. Keep being honest with yourself in the areas that need work, and don't be afraid to seek guidance. Also be very patient with those who are sharing your journey. As you learn and grow together, things will come up; insecurities will be painfully triggered. That's not a bad thing, as long as you communicate and continue to be earnest and aware of your patterns. It's the ultimate form of love you can show to one another.

When we are triggered into painful negativity, it can be easy to blame ourselves, our partner, friend, or family member. Take a step back, take a deep breath, and explore where that pain comes from. You are ok. Give yourself permission to be human and grow, and most importantly to be patient and kind with yourself. It can be very easy to be frustrated thinking that we should know better, but this is actually the perfect time to show yourself some loving compassion.

We Are Meant to Succeed

Have you ever felt whiney, angry or sad?
Or tired and frustrated and then acted mad?
You're not alone; we've all been there before
Were all out of sorts and acted quite poor.

Take heart and take heed, it's the balance of life
Some days were quite happy, others feeling some strife.
The key to this game, is to understand how it's played
When you know what to expect, your confusion will fade.

Love flows in balance; it's where we should be
Not too high, not too low, but the middle you see.
Be thankful and happy for where you are at
Life here is for learning; it's as simple as that.

So during those times when it's tough or unsure
Take a step back and think thoughts good or pure.
Remember a time when you had some success
Believe in yourself and never ever second-guess.

Your life is perfection, the good times and bad
The easy and the tough, the happy and the sad.
Each challenge brings a chance, to grow and become whole
To learn from your mistakes, and reconnect with your soul.

We are meant to succeed, so take heart and take flight
Throw out your fears and give way to love's light.
Your destiny beckons, your true nature at hand
Live life to the fullest, it's fantastic and grand!

—G. Brian Benson

Moments of Clarity

Would you consider yourself a patient person?

If not, do you see the value in being patient?

CHAPTER 18

Just Say No

no

adverb: **no**

1. a negative used to express dissent, denial, or refusal, as in response to a question or request.

   "She felt relieved after saying **no** *to the party invite."*

It's ok to say no. You knew that right? Just checking.

Let me explain how powerful this small two-letter word is. Simply put, it's an invaluable piece in your "tool bag" of mastering self-acceptance, happiness and wellbeing. If you can become adept at using no in the right situations, it will be a major contributor in your ability to stay happy, healthy and grounded.

I realize it might be hard for some of you to hear this, but you don't actually need to "save the world." It's too big of a task. If we can focus on saving ourselves first, then the world itself will begin to come into alignment. How does "saving the world" have anything to do with saying no? A lot of us choose to fix and help others instead of looking at what we need to do to fix and help ourselves. It's a defense mechanism used to avoid our own stuff. And when we do something for someone else, it gives us a moment of validation—even though it may come at our own expense.

It can be hard to say no when others come to us for help. For most of us, saying no is exceedingly difficult. I think one of the reasons we find it so hard to say no is because we want to be liked. I am no different. I am not telling you to say no to everything, and I am certainly not telling you not to be of service. But for those of you who have made it your personal mission to be saviors, let's first take a step back and ask yourself why you feel like you need to fix everything. What is missing in your life? Self-acceptance? A true love for yourself? How do I know this? Because I too used to operate from that place, being everyone's savior. I wasn't doing a proper job of taking care of my needs, nor was I accepting or loving myself enough. My sense of worthiness and esteem came from saying yes a lot. I found myself in situations or doing things that I really had no desire to do. It's a tough place to operate from. It's exhausting, actually. Saying yes to everything that comes along and constantly putting everyone else's needs in front of our own isn't sustainable. And you know what eventually happens? We start showing animosity towards those we are helping. But it's really ourselves who we are angry with. Inwardly we know we should give ourselves the love and time that we are spending on everyone else. Just remember you are worth it. Your goals and dreams are great investments and YOU deserve to honor them with your time.

I promise you, as you begin to say no you will start to feel empowered. It's not being selfish. It may feel that way initially, but you are simply taking care of your needs first. And let me remind you again that you are perfect and worthy just the way you are with what you have to work with. Other people will begin to treat you with more respect and value your time when you begin to do the same. They will feel that you are in control as your energy vibration becomes stronger.

If you want to be of service and help someone out, I think that's fantastic—and more power to you. I love to be of service as well. But check in with yourself before you say yes, and honor your true feelings. It may be a great time to help out, or you may realize that for one reason or another it isn't. It's ok to say no to the people and events that do not move you forward. No. It's the important little word with a giant impact!

Moments of Clarity

Do you find it hard to say no? If so, why?

How would your life be enhanced if you were able to say no on a more consistent basis?

CHAPTER 19

Live in the Moment

live

verb: **live**

1. to have a life rich in experience.
2. to exhibit vigor, gusto, or enthusiasm.
3. to be thoroughly absorbed by or involved with.
   "He loved to set aside his fears and **live** *in the moment!"*

Have you ever been doing something and not been totally present while you were doing it because you were worrying about something that had happened in the past or might happen in the future? Certainly we all have. When we do this, we aren't allowing ourselves to fully take in or enjoy the actual moment while it is happening. Guilt or fear can creep in and cause us much heaviness when, more often than not, there is absolutely no basis for our guilty or fearful feelings. The key when finding yourself in this situation is to remember that neither the past nor the future is real. Only the now is truly available to us. To quote John Demartini from his wonderful book *The Breakthrough Experience*, "Time consists of both future and past, neither of which can ever be in the now. The past holds memory, is emotionally based, and is dominated by the emotion labeled 'guilt.' The future holds imagination, is also emotionally based, and is dominated by the emotion labeled 'fear.' The loving essence of your true spirit is spaceless and timeless presence."

In other words, be in the caring, loving flow that life is meant to be—in the now, the place where we are able to create the life of our choosing. Where we manifest our hopes and dreams into reality. Our real self (at our core) is based in the now. So why would we ever want to do anything but live in the moment or be present?

By living in the moment, we can free ourselves from worry, guilt, fear, anger, resentment, and uncertainty. By being present we can focus on the task at hand and not on something that has already happened, or that has yet to be. The past is the past and the future has yet to be played out. And since our thoughts hold much power, we want to focus our attention on the present and be positive, not on the past where we may have experienced hurt or confusion, or the future and our potential uncertainty or fear.

I realize that this takes some work, because it can be very easy to slip into the past and play out scenarios in our mind that we may have wished hadn't happened, or had gone a different way. That is only natural, but it weakens our ability to create the now that we truly want. Try to embrace what happened in the past and be thankful for the learning experience it provided so you can move forward.

I also realize that being present isn't always easy. A dear friend recently reminded me that she didn't really want to be present as her mother was dying, but she stuck with it and stayed in the absolute NOW of the experience, even though it hurt so deeply. Being in the NOW doesn't always equal happiness, but I do think it's important to not shy away from those painful moments in our lives that are happening in the moment. Otherwise, we can never let it go. The Now is not always easy. But it's vital for us to be present so we can move forward and not get stuck and then have to relive something over and over. And please remember that when things get hard, it is temporary. When things are hard, we tend to dream of the future or romanticize the past and not be present.

For me, living in the past hasn't been where I get tripped up. It's looking forward to the future. Early on after I had written my first couple of books I felt like I was ready to be out in the world and making a bigger impact than I was, but I wasn't ready to do that. I needed some more seasoning. I needed to continue to grow and learn and solidify my foundation. It caused me a lot of frustration because I wasn't where I thought I should be, but in all truth, I was exactly where I was supposed to be. I was still the caterpillar in the cocoon not quite ready to break free and fly. And because I was looking ahead and frustrated, I missed a lot of the joy and reward of being on my journey because I wasn't living in the moment. I want you to enjoy your journey.

I had always wanted to ride my bicycle across the United States. I'm not sure when I started entertaining the idea of riding my bike across the entire country, but I think it was in college in the late 1980s. Because I had been in training for triathlons, I had been riding my bike a lot and read something in a cycling magazine about the RAAM (Race Across America) bicycle race. I didn't want to race my bike across the US, but I did think it would be fascinating to ride across it. I mean, what a great way to see the country and meet people!

In May of 1996, a friend of mine told me about Bike-Aid, a cross-country bike ride that he had participated in ten years earlier. He explained that Bike-Aid was a fundraiser for a variety of local sustainable grassroots programs in cities and towns all across America. The money that was raised would go directly to the programs that we voted on at the conclusion of the ride in Washington, DC. I knew then that this was my opportunity to live out this dream of mine. The timing was perfect and I had the summer available to make it happen. I signed up immediately and began raising the money I needed.

My preparation came together perfectly. I raised the money and I was healthy and ready to go. The starting point was in Seattle. There was a three-day orientation where I had a chance to meet the other riders in my group. There were twenty-one of us all together; a very diversified and interesting group.

As it happened, I was the second oldest rider in the group. I had just turned thirty. Most of the other cyclists were college students in their late teens or early twenties. I can't tell you how excited I was on that first day of the cross-country ride. I felt totally alive and completely present. And you know what? For the two-and-a-half-month duration of the bike ride, that feeling of being completely present and in the moment never left me. We met the most amazing and friendly people. Some of the little communities even had a potluck meal waiting for us! For about a third of the time, we stayed at local campgrounds for nightly lodging. The rest of the trip, we stayed in a variety of homes that people kindly opened up to us, as well as school gymnasiums, churches, and even a few YMCA's. We got to sleep in teepees during a two-day stay in Montana. Once a week we would stay in a town for an extra day and do a community service project. It was very rewarding. As for our daily cycling routine, we averaged about seventy-five miles a day. Some days, I would ride with a small group of my new friends. Other days, I would take off by myself and go at a speed that suited me. Each morning we were given a map/route of where we were headed for the day and folks could go at their own pace. Although I enjoyed being around others, I also appreciated my quiet time and really loved the adventurous feeling I had of riding by myself in a brand new world. I had an amazing, almost magical experience one day while I was riding solo from Glendive, Montana, to Medora, North Dakota. It was a sixty-five-mile jaunt that had me smiling like a kid in a candy store. I had the pleasure of having the strongest tailwind pushing me from behind that I had ever experienced. I made the sixty-five-mile ride in only two hours! Although I was a strong and experienced rider, I had never ever come close to averaging 32.5 miles per hour for that long of a ride. I was in cycling nirvana that day.

We took the Northern route across the US, and had countless opportunities to experience things that I never would have dreamed of. In Yellowstone National Park, I saw moose just a few feet away and also a grizzly bear running across a meadow about three hundred yards away. It was both awe-inspiring and a bit scary, since I was on my bike! The steep climb up and over 10,947-foot Bear Tooth Pass, just outside of Yellowstone, was remarkable and I loved every minute of it! We stayed on the Lame Deer Reservation in Montana. It was an absolute honor learning about their proud history and touring the surrounding countryside. We also happened to be there during a large Pow-Wow celebration. There was music and dancing throughout the days and nights that we were guests. I can still taste the delicious fry bread.

I truly enjoyed catching baseball games at both Wrigley Field in Chicago and Three Rivers Stadium in Pittsburgh. Baseball is a special game to me. There's no clock. One can truly get lost in time and forget about all that is going on while taking in a live ballgame. It's a wonderful exercise of staying present in the moment, just like I was doing on this trip. The clean air, the smell of the grass, and the popcorn; the shouts of the vendor and announcer all bring back fond memories for me.

Riding my bicycle through the historic grounds of both Little Bighorn Battlefield and Antietam National Battlefield were also very powerful, almost spiritual journeys for me. Moving slowly through those now-beautiful parks, one can really feel the unsettled and disconcerting energy of battle and of those that went before.

And last but certainly not least, there was the nude ride. First of all, let me tell you that there is nothing more invigorating, life affirming, scary, and self-questioning than riding one's bike nude in public. I found myself in this thrilling, yet odd position basically because I had to make a quick choice. This particular choice for me was between eternal regret and some potential embarrassment or lifelong glory and a great story to share with friends and family around future campfires.

On the very last day of our cross-country journey, as we rode the thirty-five miles from Leesburg, Virginia, to Washington, DC, some of the riders stopped while we were riding along a bike path. Feeling curious, I stopped to ask what was up. I soon found out that part of the group wanted to do a nude bike ride to celebrate. As soon as I heard "nude bike ride" I began to get butterflies in my stomach. In my mind, I knew I had to do it. I was never one to step away from a dare or a challenge. I also knew that we would be seen by a lot of people that were either walking/jogging on the path or driving their cars to and fro on the outskirts of the Nation's capital. And of course I also knew that I would regret not doing this for the rest of my life if I didn't join up. I had to make a quick choice because they had already started to take off their clothes. If I were to go all-in and do this, I certainly didn't want to be left behind riding naked by myself while trying to catch up. I wanted to blend in with the rest of the group and not get stuck at a crosswalk during a red light all by myself! Without any time to lose, I swallowed hard, took a deep breath and stripped down to nothing and joined the rest of the crazies.

All I can tell you about the two- or three-mile naked ride (other than it went by in a blur), is that seeing the reaction of the people that we passed on the bike trail and intersections were totally priceless. Some folks were laughing out loud; some folks looked like they had just seen a ghost, while the majority just had a look of puzzlement on their face. It was awesome. Talk about living in the moment! My only mistake was giving my bike clothes to my friend Jeff who wasn't joining in with us. He purposely held back a bit so that when we were done, I had to wait a couple of minutes for him to catch up before I could get dressed. That was the worst part of the whole experience. The funny thing is I would have done the same thing to him.

Everything about my Seattle to DC experience was perfect; the people, the memories, the reason we were doing it, and the beautiful landscape. People are friendly and kind at their core and I was blessed to have been able to see people from all over our country at their finest. During this trip I learned what it was like to truly *live in the moment*. I am forever grateful.

Moments of Clarity

Do you find it easy to stay in the present moment or do you find yourself focusing on the past or future?

Or both?

If so, why?

CHAPTER 20

Go Love and Be Loved

love

noun: love

1. a feeling of warm personal attachment or deep affection, as for a parent, child, or friend.
2. a profoundly tender, passionate affection for another person.
   "She felt a genuine **love** *from her friends."*

Love is a word that has so many layers of meaning. Yet when it is used in the context of "finding love" or "falling in love" a lot of us tend to picture the rosy little bubble of the perfect Hollywood movie ending. There are so many ways to share and fall in love, yet we have been trained it has to look a certain way. And while the perfect Hollywood ending would be awesome and amazing, it holds many of us hostage from exploring and finding love because we hold out for the perfect situation, person or ending. And to be honest, I don't think it necessary exists like we are meant to believe. I will tell you what does exist, and that is that there are millions of people out there walking around who want to love and be loved that aren't allowing themselves to be because it's not showing up like they expect it.

Love isn't a mythical romantic movie formula but a progression of individual moments that move us toward a deeper level of love. It could be with one person for the long term or it could be with a number of people as we chart our path and continue to grow. Love expresses itself in many different ways.

If you hold out forever waiting for "the one" you may never find any form of love at all. And that is really sad because love is our true essence and we are wired to be in it, move through it and resonate to its vibration. So why not practice and allow it to flow in its many different forms. If it is meant to last with a particular person then it will last, if not, that's okay too. You will have learned more about yourself at a deeper level.

Allow yourself moments each and every day to open up your heart and share love with yourself, a friend, someone you just met or your partner. That will open up your channels and lend yourself to a higher vibration of love in all its many wonderful splendid forms. Just like the Crosby, Stills and Nash song says, "love the one you're with." Set your fears, expectations, and judgments aside and open your heart up to others. Let go of your old stories of what love is and how it should play out.

Loving moments or the potential for loving moments are all around us every single day. Immerse yourself in them, allow yourself to be vulnerable, let go of the expectation of where they might lead. That just takes us out of being in the moment. Let it unfold naturally. Trying to control the situation will only lessen the joy of the moment as well as potentially sever the connection. Allow yourself to learn and grow with an open heart as you gain self-awareness through a loving, communicative openness.

I am a giver by nature and for the longest time seemed to have one half of the puzzle solved. I had no trouble giving and sharing with others, but wasn't able to receive and let others love me. I remember one time while I was in Toastmasters; one of the other members complimented me on how I looked. I immediately began to negate what she said by putting myself down and offering up something like "Oh, this old shirt?" or "Really? I have had these clothes for ever." Wrong answer! She told me that by responding like I did, I took away her joy that came along with paying me a compliment. She finished by saying that receiving a compliment is just as important as giving one. That was a big lesson for me. Allowing ourselves to be complimented is another way to allow ourselves to be loved. And that is extremely powerful. As I now move through my life I am much more aware that to love fully means to be able to let others love me as well. And I am not just talking about a romantic relationship. It could simply mean allowing someone to buy you lunch or give you a token of their appreciation. Early on, every time someone wanted to do something for me I felt like I had to immediately reciprocate the gesture. By refusing or trying to make things equal on the spot I was doing two things. First of all I was hijacking the joy of the other person during their moment of wanting to share. Secondly, I continued to reinforce the false story that I was not worthy of receiving. An open heart doesn't have to be a one-way street. A flow back and forth, giving and receiving is incredibly important and we are all worthy of experiencing both. Find love, share love and be in love with yourself and others. It is the cornerstone of your foundation. You deserve it.

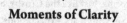

Moments of Clarity

What areas of love do you allow in?

Where might it be missing?

CHAPTER 21

Continue to Learn and Grow

grow

verb: **grow**

1. to increase by natural development.
2. to increase gradually in size, amount, etc.; become greater or larger; expand.

   "His daughter loved school because it allowed her to learn and grow."

It's important to always be willing to continue to learn and grow. Life is constantly flowing and evolving around us. I feel we should be doing the same. We aren't meant to be stagnant. Life is so much richer when we continue to grow, mature, and have new experiences. I know it isn't always easy, but that's what makes it so fulfilling; to continue to test ourselves and see the world with new eyes.

There are so many ways to learn and grow. Let's start with my favorite, the self-growth process. I find nothing more inspiring than to witness someone who wants to do the work to be a better version of themselves. I know how hard I have worked at my own process and also the rewards that it can bring. I want everyone to experience the joy, fulfillment and feeling of the accomplishment of self-awareness. I have found that self-awareness leads to self-love; the ultimate gift we can give ourselves. The sky's the limit with an open mind, open heart and the willingness to learn.

When we continue to learn and grow, new pathways are opened up, new ways of thinking are offered, our foundation is strengthened and experiences we may have only dreamed of prior are available. Here are some great ways to open yourself up to new experiences.

- *Take a class.* Find a subject that interests you and expand your knowledge.

- *Learn a new language.* What a great way to enhance a potential trip that is coming up! Go and learn some of the language of where you are visiting. I was so glad I took a few community college French language classes before I went over to visit Europe many years back.

- *Read a book.* I think when someone said, "good things come in small packages," they were definitely referring to books. Books are an incredible way to not only free your mind, but also to fill it with knowledge, adventure and inspiration at the same time. Nothing like expanding your horizons getting lost in a book!

- *Ask questions.* There is no such thing as a dumb question. Ask away. Learn about others and how things work!

- *Pay attention to your surroundings.* Keep your head up and look around as you are walking or driving. You never know what you might see. I love to walk neighborhoods and cities. I have been able to learn so much just through observation.

- *Pick up an instrument.* Tap into a potential hidden talent! Pick up the guitar or piano or harmonica or...

- *Take a trip.* There is so much to be seen and learned outside of our usual environs. Take a day trip and see what lay just beyond your neck of the woods. Take a trip to another country and really pique your curiosity.

- *Try a new sport.* It's never too late to pick up a new sport. Go take some golf or tennis lessons. They are great forms of exercise and ways to share in some fun.

- *Try some new foods.* Step out of your routine a bit and delve into some new delicacies. You will feel adventurous and maybe find some new favorites.

- *Have a conversation with a senior citizen.* Our elders have so much experience, wisdom and joy to share. Why wouldn't you want to hear their stories and learn about their experiences?

These are all beautiful and wonderful ways to learn and grow. It's important to being open to having new experiences.

I want to share a personal example. After having made it through my first two years of racing in triathlons, I knew that I enjoyed it immensely and that it gave me a lot of confidence and pride. I still wanted to improve though. I was working as a lifeguard at Oregon State University and noticed the women's swim team come in one time following a class I watched over. That got me thinking. I felt that while I was an ok swimmer I knew that my swimming could stand some improvement. I had heard that the women's team was a funded university sport and I found out that they also had a men's swim club that wasn't. It was participant funded. I then began to wonder who was on the men's team and could anyone join? After some inquiries, I realized that anyone could join. I knew right then and there that was my answer to become a better swimmer; I joined. I didn't really know at the time what I was getting myself into. My triathlon swim training basically consisted of me jumping in the pool and swimming lap after lap. Maybe I would throw in some kickboard work. That was about it.

That was all about to change very quickly at swim practice. Everybody who was on the team had been a very proficient swimmer in high school and was quite fast and talented. Here I was, someone whose swim career consisted of a handful of triathlons and some summer swim lessons as a youth. I was terrified. Luckily for me the coach of the team was a supportive and wise man who had been coaching for a very long time. He understood where I was coming from and welcomed me.

No more jumping in the pool and swimming lap after lap for me. It was time for lung burning intervals and trying swim strokes which I had never attempted before. That first day while struggling my way through practice, I really began to wonder what I got myself into. Although quitting was an option that I honestly did think about, I decided to go again the next day. The routine was the same, lung-busting interval after lung-busting interval, but I began to realize that I could handle it. Sure I was the slowest swimmer there, but I knew that I could handle it. I also began to realize that there was no way I couldn't get faster if I stuck with this. So that is what I did. Although practices were always tough, I began to get faster and more confident day after day. It was a wonderful feeling indeed. I even went on road trips with them to swim meets and competed in the freestyle events (that was the stroke used for triathlon). Although I got my butt kicked in the meets by all the experienced swimmers, it was exhilarating and a lot of fun being a part of the team. The next summer during triathlon race season, I turned in some great swim times, which felt really good. I was incredibly proud of myself for giving it a go and being willing to learn. I want you to feel the same way.

Moments of Clarity

When was the last time you opened yourself up to learn something new?

Where are some areas where you might enjoy learning something new?

CHAPTER 22

Be Inspired

in·spi·red

adjective: **inspired**

1. aroused, animated, or imbued with the spirit to do something, by or as if by supernatural or divine influence.
    *"She felt **inspired** to go watch the sunset."*

I love to be inspired. There is nothing quite like having my heart and senses come alive while feeling the beautiful flow of being touched by something inspirational. I am sure you would agree. I try to surround myself with as much beauty as I possibly can. I find that it helps me stay aware and connected with the love, beauty and wholeness that reside within all of us. Being inspired also reminds me of the goodness that I can find in other people. To be inspired is to have your entire being wake up and say, "I can do this!" I find that when I am inspired I am also reminded of our connection to one another. We are not separate beings; we are unified at our core. We all want to love and be loved.

There are so many ways to bring inspiration into our lives. One of the easiest is to watch an inspirational show or movie. It's a guaranteed fix to get you feeling upbeat, motivated and aligned. They allow us to dream and believe that anything is possible. There are many other ways to be inspired:

- *Go visit a museum.* I enjoy history and art. There is nothing I love more than to visit a museum and learn about the past and view its beauty.

- *Spend some time in nature.* I truly love hiking and spending time in nature. To me nature is perfection. When I am out in the woods, my mind becomes clear and everything feels like it is going to be all right.

- *Watch a professional sporting event.* Go watch the best athletes in the world compete at the highest level. Having grown up playing sports and being a pretty good athlete, I sit in amazement, joy and admiration while watching a game.

- *Meditate.* I love meditation and the many forms that it presents itself. My creative abilities come alive while sitting in silence. Did you know that walking, exercise, playing and listening to certain types of music can be forms of meditation as well?

- *Listen to live music.* I feel listening to and watching talented musicians play live is one of life's greatest joys.

- *Sit under the stars.* Look up in wonder at the vastly beautiful Universe that surrounds us. It really puts things into perspective.

- *Hang out with positive people.* What is better than having an engaging conversation and surrounding yourself with like-minded, positive people? I always feel energized and better after connecting with others.

- *Be of service.* I think being of service is an important part of our ability to find true happiness and fulfillment in our lives. I always feel inspired after helping others.

One of my favorite things to do is to walk or drive around Los Angeles and view street art. I find it fascinating, creative and uplifting. I try and find inspiration almost everywhere, especially in the stories of others. If you truly think about it, every single person has a story to tell. And our personal stories link us together through vulnerability, courage and love. If we paid attention and listened to one another's stories, I think it would eliminate much of the fear, ignorance and hate in our world.

I remember feeling quite touched a couple of years back when I watched the documentary *Emmanuel's Gift.* If you haven't seen it, I highly recommend it; it will change your life. It is about a young Ghanaian man named Emmanuel Ofosu Yeboah. Emmanuel was born without a tibia in one of his legs. Because of his birth defect, he struggled to do all of the things those of us with two working legs might take for granted. Emmanuel had to resort to crawling and using crutches most of his life because his right leg was severely deformed and unusable. But that didn't stop him from wanting to make a difference.

To raise awareness for the two million disabled and neglected people in Ghana (or 10 percent of Ghana's total population), he bravely wrote the Challenged Athletes Foundation (CAF) based in San Diego and asked for a bike so he could bicycle across the country of Ghana (with one leg). The CAF granted Emmanuel's wish, sent him a bike and he set out on his journey of 360 miles across the country of Ghana. What transpired was amazing. Local radio and television picked up on his quest and soon the whole country became involved. The local rulers and politicians could no longer turn a blind eye to the disabled of their country. Emmanuel's grit and heart made tremendous inroads into how the disabled in Ghana are treated today.

After watching the documentary I was inspired to write to Emmanuel in Ghana and ask if I could donate some athletic gear for a foundation that he established for athletes with disabilities. He kindly wrote back and welcomed anything that I could put together. I then connected with many of my local triathlon friends and had them donate some gear as well. With an inspired heart, I shipped off three boxes of clothes and goods to Ghana. Shortly thereafter I received a phone call from Emmanuel. I was surprised to say the least. After profusely thanking me for the clothes, he mentioned that he currently happened to be in San Diego raising funds and collecting bicycles to send back to his foundation in Ghana. I asked him how I could help. I happened to be living in Reno, Nevada, at the time (about a ten-hour drive away) and felt like I really wanted to meet this inspiring person. He graciously invited me down to visit. I then went on Craig's List to try and collect some used bikes in Reno that I could put in my car to take down with me when I visited. I ended up finding seven bikes that I miraculously fit into my Honda Element and made the drive down to San Diego. Emmanuel couldn't have been more kind and humble. He is a truly inspiring man embracing his life's purpose. It was a real pleasure to be able to share a dinner, connect and make a new friend. This is a wonderful case of inspiration creating inspiration. Allow yourself to be inspired and watch your world open up. Inspiration opens the door to our souls.

Moments of Clarity

What inspires you?

How could you bring more of what inspires you into your life?

CHAPTER 23

Clean Up Your Disagreements

dis·a·gree·ment

noun: **disagreement**

1. quarrel; dissension; argument.
2. the act, state, or fact of disagreeing.
   "He felt bad when the **disagreements** *turned angry."*

"To err is human, to forgive is divine." Ah, the wise words of Alexander Pope. Do you have unresolved issues hanging over you? I would venture to say that we all have had unresolved issues at one time or another: a misunderstanding with a family member or friend, or possibly a disagreement with a co-worker. We are human, it happens. But to truly free ourselves of the pain, anger, guilt, or confusion we are holding onto, we need to make our best effort to clear things up. Which means either to forgive the other person and move on or try to patch things up so you can go back to being friends or productive coworkers. This is so important for our mental, emotional and physical wellbeing. Not to mention the strength of our foundation.

Someone may have done a really hurtful thing to you and it's no fun to be on the receiving end of that. I know because I have been there myself. The act can be debilitating. It took me almost thirty years to forgive the four guys who bullied me when I was on the JV high school baseball team. I was a sophomore at the time playing primarily with older guys and one of them jokingly thought I looked like a monkey. So he and a few others proceeded to call me that during the entire baseball season and school year. What they said hurt me to the core and made me question my attractiveness for the first half of my life. It also played a big part in my own self-worth process or should I say lack of self-worth. It may seem crazy because I was successful in a lot of areas of my life, yet I still felt unworthy at a deeper level. Eventually I realized I had to try and forgive them. It took the power out of their hurtful words and helped me begin to truly love myself. It was a gift that I had to give to myself. I feel that we can begin to let go of the anger and hurt even if we are not totally ready to forgive.

I realize there are all kinds of problems and misunderstandings. Some problems are much bigger than others. And some misunderstandings will not be as easily rectified either. There are some situations that are really hard to forgive…child abuse, rape, violence, certain kinds of betrayal…that said, we could begin to let go and release the burden and not let that define who we are. Some situations may require outside help such as a therapist, mediator or trusted friend. However, each situation that is resolved, no matter how big or small, is one more step towards freedom.

You owe it to yourself to remove the burden. Or at least begin to remove the burden. Our true nature is one of love and connection. That's why it hurts so much when there is disconnect. Forgiveness is the single hardest thing that keeps us from thriving and not just surviving. Forgive and free yourself.

To forgive and let go is the greatest gift
You can give yourself to watch your spirit lift
Your life will move forward with the past behind
No obstructions, just production with a free flowing mind

—**G. Brian Benson** (*stanza from poem "Keys to Life"*)

Moments of Clarity

Are there any people that you could forgive or begin to forgive? If not, are there other ways you can free yourself from the hurt or pain?

How about yourself? Is there any part of your past actions where you could make amends or forgive yourself?

CHAPTER 24

Have Faith and Trust the Process

pro·cess

noun: process
1. a continuous action, operation, or series of changes
    taking place in a definite manner.
2. a systematic series of actions directed to some end.
    "Patience during her **process** *wasn't easy, but it was
    rewarding."*

We are constantly learning and growing. However, sometimes we aren't
quite ready for a task even though we might think we are. Case in point. I have
always felt like I was destined to help others. When I was three years old, I told
my mother I was "put here to inspire people." And when my path actually began
to unfold that way after I left my family business I felt like I was ready to do it
on a larger-scale, long before I really was. For example, whenever I created and
released a project (book, film, video etc.), in the back of my mind I would be
thinking, "Is this going to be my big break?" Looking back its quite embarrassing,
believe me, but it took a lot of faith and trusting the process to keep moving
forward. I mean I was really working hard and investing a lot of my time, heart
and personal finances into my projects. I began to feel my inner flame, which had
burned so bright full of motivation at the beginning of my journey slowly begin
to diminish. I would often wonder, "How long do I have to keep proving myself?"
Looking back I realize, I needed to go through all of what I went through, all
of the lessons, hardships, ups and downs and unfulfilled expectations. This
incredible rollercoaster ride of events, trials and experiences made me who I am
today and have given me the tools to be able to truly help others because I also
have been scared, become vulnerable, suffered, grown and overcome. It's a bond
that we all share. Please stay focused, hold trust and keep moving forward. You
will get there my friend.

Did you know I first started writing my first children's book *Steve the Alien* back in
2004? I wrote the first half of the story yet couldn't quite figure out how to finish
it. I set it down for three years and picked it back up and finished it in 2007. I then

signed a contract with a company in 2010 that was going to make *Steve the Alien* into a moving picture book for a children's app. I was thrilled! Then after about a year and a half, the company ran out of money and *Steve the Alien* was shelved again. Needless to say I was very disappointed. After getting them to release me from the contract the story sat another five years before I got the courage to find an illustrator and create the story on my own by self-publishing in 2016. On its launch day, it even reached Amazon bestseller status and hit number one in its category. I was certainly surprised and very proud that I hung in there and brought it to fruition thirteen years after I began writing it. *Steve the Alien* was a project that always gave me a lot of joy while writing it and I had hoped way back then that I would be able to see this rhyming adventure spring to life in vivid illustrations one day. It was certainly worth the wait. It's never too late to make something happen, I just needed to have faith and trust the process.

Andre Ingram was a thirty-two-year-old professional basketball player who had never made it to the National Basketball Association, the top tier of professional basketball. After playing college basketball for American University and graduating in 2007 with a physics degree, Andre wasn't drafted by an NBA team and began playing minor league professional basketball in the G league.

Andre believed in his abilities and loved basketball so much that he forgo making a lot more money utilizing his physics degree and settled for the G league salary of around $25,000 a year having to supplement his income by becoming a math tutor to support his family.

Andre's dream of playing in the NBA was so strong that he continued playing in the G league for ten years. Normally players will stick around for a few years hoping for a call up and when it doesn't happen usually either retire or go play professionally overseas for more money. Andre didn't do either of those things. He continued to believe that he was good enough to play in the NBA. He endured long bus rides; he played in front of small crowds in even smaller cities. He and his family had to truly sacrifice to make ends meet.

Until finally on April 9, 2018 Andre received a call from the Los Angeles Lakers who wanted to sign him for the final two games of the season. Andre's dream came true. Andre scored nineteen points in his NBA debut making all but two of his shots. At thirty-two years old, Andre became the oldest American rookie in the NBA since 1964. It was an incredible accomplishment born out of dogged determination, incredible fortitude and an unyielding belief in himself. Andre had faith and trusted the process.

Some Other Benefits of Being Patient and Trusting the Process

- You open yourself up to potentially better timing.
- You will appear more professional and trustworthy to others.
- It feels better because you earned it.
- Things won't feel forced. You will have a more stable and calm resonance.
- You will have built a more sustainable and healthier foundation.
- You won't risk suffering from remorse.
- You won't risk the embarrassment of not appearing ready.
- It takes potentially needy or unhealthy energy out of the equation.
- If it's meant to be, it will be.

Moments of Clarity

Are you able to trust your process?

If not, why?

How would your life be different if you were able to be more patient?

CHAPTER 25

Keep Up Your Momentum

mo·men·tum

noun: **momentum**

1. strength or force gained by motion or by a series of events.
   "The wagon gained **momentum** *as it rolled down the hill."*

Momentum is such an important tool in our desire to grow, succeed, and solidify our foundations. When it flows, life feels easy and rich, but when it doesn't we feel like we are knee-deep in quicksand with no hope for rescue. I get it. That's why it's so important to keep moving forward if we can, even if it's a baby step.

How do we keep it going? Through diligence, awareness, and routine. Momentum plays a huge part in whether you will achieve your goals, especially if it is something that took courage for you to begin in the first place. With lost momentum, loss of focus usually follows. You have to keep the flow going or before you know it, a few days go by and it becomes even more difficult to resume your practice. This applies to almost anything; writing a book, sticking to a diet plan, exercise or cleaning out the garage. If you miss a couple of days, there's a chance you lose your nerve and decide not to show up anymore. Which means it will be doubly hard to start that goal again in the future because you will have attached a seed of failure to your experience. But on the other hand if you keep it up, your confidence will continue to expand which will make it easier to begin future goals.

I can attest to the importance of maintaining a routine to help keep your momentum flowing. My routine of establishing balance with daily exercise, good nutrition, proper sleep and meditation (areas I will cover later in the book) has helped me maintain the energy, creativity and desire to keep moving forward even when things get tough. Momentum becomes much more difficult when we are scrambling about not sure which way to proceed.

Not too long ago there was a car parked out in front of my home for five days. It had a flat tire. Having a car parked in front of my residence was nothing new. It was normal to have cars come and go from that spot; I got used to the variety and the flow. Seeing that same car day after day, coupled with the fact that it had a flat tire, began to make me feel uncomfortable. Each day thereafter, noticing its presence made me wish it wasn't there. Interestingly enough, I didn't feel that way with the other cars that parked there; maybe because I knew they were temporary. It made me feel like the energy of the parking spot was always in flow. So on day five when I noticed that the car was finally gone, I let out a sigh of relief. And that got me thinking, why did the anchored car bother me?

I then remembered that everything consists of energy, and energy needs to be fluid. Because we are part of that equation, we struggle when we stay stagnant and immobile. If we don't allow ourselves to breathe, flex our muscles, and grow, it feels unnatural and joyless. That's why it's so important to keep expanding and to keep our momentum in flow. Don't be like the static car in the parking spot too long. How's that for a metaphor?

Moments of Clarity

Have there been times when you have lost momentum?

What can you do to make sure that doesn't happen again in the future?

LIGHT BULB MOMENTS

Be Kind, Generous, and Giving

Our prime purpose in this life is to help others. And if you can't help them, at least don't hurt them.

—The Dalai Lama

I've learned that people will forget what you said, people will forget what you did, but people will never forget how you made them feel.

— Maya Angelou

Sometimes when we are generous in small, barely detectable ways it can change someone else's life forever.

— Margaret Cho

I believe that we all have a responsibility to give back. No one becomes successful without lots of hard work, support from others, and a little luck. Giving back creates a virtuous cycle that makes everyone more successful.

— Ron Conway

The full measure of our personal happiness is dictated by how much we offer of ourselves in helping others.

— G. Brian Benson

I've been searching for ways to heal myself, and I've found that kindness is the best way.

—Lady Gaga

Volunteering is a great way to look outside your own problems. Giving back to others makes you happier by both giving you a sense of purpose and helping to put your problems in perspective.

—Karen Salmansohn

We make a living by what we get. We make a life by what we give.

—Winston Churchill

Tenderness and kindness are not signs of weakness and despair, but manifestations of strength and resolution.

— Kahlil Gibran

Courage, kindness, friendship, character. These are the qualities that define us as human beings, and propel us, on occasion, to greatness.

—R. J. Palacio

If you have more than you need, bless someone else who has less.

—Unknown

CHAPTER 26

Go Play

play

noun: **play**

1. exercise or activity for amusement or recreation.
   "The child loved to **play** *in the sandbox."*

Remember when you were a kid? If you were anything like me, you were lost in a land of make believe, playing a myriad of games and having loads of fun getting absorbed in the moment. Think back for a second and try to place yourself back on that prized bicycle or in that special tree house. Can you resonate with that feeling? How does it feel? There really is nothing like playing with your childhood friends without a worry in the world. Can you feel the lightness of the moment? Can you feel your worries just drift away? Can you feel the excited optimism and happiness that comes from hanging around your friends? It drifts in and out, back and forth while the warm sun stands watch over whatever game you happen to be playing that day.

This carefree lifestyle we led as kids; this carefree feeling that anything was possible. Where did it go? You know there is no reason that you can't tap back into that feeling. Just because you are older doesn't mean that it has to be lost forever. We can learn a lot from children and how they carry themselves. In all actuality, I think that to be able to regain that carefree, happy, optimistic, anything is possible feeling we had as kids is not only possible to regain, but it is a key component in maintaining our happiness, having a fulfilled life and creating and living out our goals and dreams.

I am so glad that I grew up when I did. Video games hadn't quite yet become the norm and cell phones were still about ten years away. I used to come home and play baseball with a handful of my friends each day after school. If I wasn't doing that I was probably shooting baskets or jumping my dirt bike over a shallow ditch. I loved sports and I truly just loved to play. I think we need to do more of it.

I realize that not everyone had ideal childhoods and I have empathy and a warm spot in my heart for you. But I just want to remind you that it's never too late to learn how to play regardless of your childhood. It's never too late to recapture the joy that lies in allowing yourself to explore, get dirty and laugh. I challenge you to open yourself up to the possibilities.

How do we tap back into this feeling? How do we regain that carefree nature that is open to possibility and being lost in the moment that kids have mastered? Here are some suggestions…

Go play a game. Grab a Frisbee and some friends and throw it around. Play a board game with your grandkids. Go shoot baskets at the local park basketball hoop. It doesn't matter what it is, just go play; get lost in the moment.

Let go of the urge to "do." Let go of feeling like you always have to go do something. Sure we all have responsibilities as we get older, family, work, etc. But I am a firm believer that we create a lot of habits that aren't really that important. Identify them and let them go. Watching too much TV? Spending too much time on the Internet? Take some of that wasted time and go play! Not only will you gain the benefits of playing but you will also release some of the weight and pressure of your perceived "need" to do something.

Be in the moment. Leave your to-do list and phone at home. Just focus on what you are doing at that very moment. Let tomorrow's tasks stay in the future.

Hang around fun, positive people. It's as simple as it sounds. Surround yourself with folks that already get it. If you are hanging out with fun, positive people it is only natural that some of their energy and fun nature rubs off on you!

Be open-minded. Let go of any preconceived notions you have about yourself and what you are doing while you are playing. Many of us try so hard to maintain certain images of ourselves that keep us rigid, sometimes stuck and closed-minded. Be open to trying new things; be open to looking silly sometimes. It can be very freeing.

Take a trip back down memory lane and see, feel and remember what it was like to truly play. Not only will it provide you with a new sense of purpose, but also help you lead a much happier and healthier life. Tag your it!

Play

Light shines in and hearts open wide
As we follow bliss, let it guide

To reach new heights and comfort zones
Release the weight, pay off the loans

That hold us back, when we don't play
Instant freedom, each brand new day

Colors seem brighter, goodness grows
A smile drifts, from our head to toes

Worries are tabled, fears subside
Troublesome thoughts go off and hide

Our mind is empty, freedom complete
Chance to renew, loving retreat

Creative flow, from higher realms
Speak truth through us and take the helm

In tune, aware, to every sound
No more searching, our soul is found

True prescription, in every way
To soar and be free, simply play

—G. Brian Benson

Moments of Clarity

Do you allow yourself to play?

What are some things that you could do that would be considered playful?

CHAPTER 27

Create Awareness

a·ware·ness

noun: **awareness**

1. the state or condition of being aware; having knowledge; consciousness.
2. knowledge and understanding that something is happening or exists.

   *"He seemed to have only a slight **awareness** of what was going on."*

Knowledge is power, pure and simple. As we learn, grow, and become more self-aware our world opens up in amazing ways. We stop repeating harmful, never-ending cycles, we let go of others who aren't impacting our life in a positive, loving way and we get unstuck from our inaction of not knowing our true path. The beauty of being self-aware is that it is an ongoing process. We are here to learn and grow and when we are open to that task our lives become much more enjoyable and free.

There is always a wealth of information coming through us at any given time. When we can identify the areas where we keep running into problems we can then take a step back to figure out what it's about and why it keeps popping up. The intention is that by becoming aware of our limiting patterns, we can stop the same recurrences of pain from happening in the future. This pain may occur for a variety of reasons. We let ego get in the way, we might be playing the victim card, our own negative self-talk, the company we keep or even because of our own lack of self-esteem. The good news is that these are all areas we can improve on.

- Self-awareness helps us maintain healthier relationships with others and ourselves.

- Self-awareness helps us understand the origins of our fears.

- Self-awareness helps us release that which doesn't serve us.

- Self-awareness allows us to truly take flight and move towards our goals and dreams.

As I work on my own self-awareness, I try to be in what I call the "observer" role. What this means is that I simply step outside of myself and observe my daily interactions from a distance—like someone standing next to me who is watching me in action. It helps me be rational and get to the core of the areas where I need to be more self-aware in. I pay attention to where I get triggered and then try to figure out why. I draw on past experiences, which I have filed away, and allow myself to be open, to listen, to be present. This knowledge helps me be more attentive and ultimately a better version of myself. Stuff happens to all of us, but it is our level of self-awareness that allows us to move through it more comfortably. Awareness is the first step toward our personal freedom.

The Man and His Horse

A monk slowly walks along a road when he hears the sound of a galloping horse. He turns around to see a man riding a horse moving in his direction. When the man comes closer, the monk asks, "Where are you going?" To which the man replies, "I don't know, ask the horse," and rides away.

Moral of the Story

The horse in the story represents your subconscious mind. The subconscious mind runs on past conditioning. It is nothing but a computer program. If you are lost in the program, the program controls you and leads you wherever it feels like.

Instead, when you become self-aware, you start to become aware of your programs and start looking at them objectively. Once you become aware of the program, you start to control the program and not the other way round.

Written by Mukesh Mani

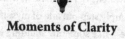

Moments of Clarity

How self-aware would you consider yourself to be?

Where are some areas that you would like to be more self-aware?

What habits could you practice to maintain your awareness?

CHAPTER 28

Always Do Your Best Work

work

noun: work

1. exertion or effort directed to produce or accomplish something; labor; toil.
2. productive or operative activity.
   "She seemed to do her best **work** *in the morning."*

"The best preparation for good work tomorrow is to do good work today," according to Elbert Hubbard. I agree, always do your best work. It's as simple as it sounds, right? It may be simple, but it's not always that easy. We tend to complicate things, make excuses, take short cuts, get things done as fast as we can. Is that our best work? What does always doing your best mean to you? Does it make you feel that you need to create perfection, or meet high expectations or strive for achievement? I completely understand that. I used to think that way too. Doing our best isn't about perfection, success or failure. Perfection doesn't exist. It's a mindset that can get in the way and rob us of any joy or fulfillment that we should be taking from a project or experience.

According to writer, David Erichsen, "Doing your best is synonymous with living out each and every moment to its fullest potential. And this potential exists in every situation you encounter in your life. Doing your best is simply about taking pride in knowing that you gave it your all while putting all of your energy and resources into your project." I wholeheartedly agree.

I know this is going to sound like proud papa time, but I have always been inspired by my son Michael's work ethic and attention to detail. He is a very talented photographer/videographer as well as an incredibly creative craftsman (welding and woodwork). All of the work that he produces is superior and he takes pride in doing the job right as well as taking care of his equipment. While he and I both have creative abilities, they are about as varied as our height difference (he is 6'2" and I am 5' 8"). There is no way I could do what he does and he would probably say the same thing about what I do.

I asked him how he developed his valuable habits. He told me that it originally stemmed from his desire to be original with his work and go the extra mile to stand out. When he was younger, he would watch other people doing jobs that he wanted to do (photography/videography) in the action sports world (primarily snowboarding) and it would motivate him to learn all that he could about those jobs, the people, and the equipment, He would then identify the areas where they were falling short. He would really prepare and work harder than others while keeping true to his vision, which in turn created his own unique style. He jokingly told me that he was like a Ninja and that his equipment was like his battle sword and he needed to keep it in tip top shape to do his best work. He definitely brings intensity to what he does. He prides himself in thinking outside of the box and constantly asks, "How can I do it different, or better?" He also feels that it is extremely important to face your weaknesses so that you can strive to strengthen them, definitely good advice. He also shared that what ultimately motivates him is the internal achievement; pride in doing a unique job and the creativity it takes to produce it.

Whatever you do my friend, always do your best work.

Why is it important to do your best work?

- It will train you to be the best version of yourself.

- It will help you develop good habits.

- It will show others that you care, are reliable and produce quality.

- It will help you build trust with others.

- It will lead to other opportunities.

- It will help you learn how to do things the right way, and there's often more than one right way.

- You will feel pride in knowing that you gave it your all.

Moments of Clarity

Do you take pride in your work?

Do you try to do your best? If not, why?

CHAPTER 29

Be of Service

ser·vice

noun: service

1. an act of helpful activity.
2. contribution to the welfare of others.

   *"Acts of **service** are a great way to bring people together."*

How do you feel when you help someone out? It feels good, right? It doesn't matter if you are helping a friend move or spending an afternoon at the local food bank. It just feels good! I have always said that the full measure of our personal happiness is dictated by how much we offer of ourselves in helping others. It's simple: be of service. Giving can occur in many different ways:

- Volunteer your time.

- Be a coach for a youth sports league.

- Read to children in a school-sponsored program.

- Be a friend to seniors at an assisted living facility.

- Help someone who is struggling to get back on his or her feet.

- Mentor a teenager through the many different and wonderful programs available.

I remember how rewarding it was for me to be part of the Big Brothers/Big Sisters program while I was in college. They matched me with a really great kid who was in middle school. Once a week we would hang out and shoot baskets or play catch. We both shared a love of sports. The experience was a lot of fun and it felt really good to help out and be a role model. It was something I always looked forward to doing.

A few years later I took it a step further and mentored a young man who was in juvenile prison. I also met with him once a week to chat, hang out and eat dinner. It was a very sobering and rewarding experience. Really made me appreciative of my upbringing. He and the rest of his cottage group were all excited that I would come and spend time with them. They all wanted the same thing that we do; love, validation and connection. There are folks everywhere who could use a mentor or a support system. And the time you invest is really inconsequential. The couple of hours a week that you donate your time will come back to you tenfold—I guarantee.

If you have the means, there are countless of worthy programs that depend on private funding to run their operations. Food kitchens for the homeless, wheelchair programs for the disabled, sports programs for youth, public radio—and that's just the tip of the iceberg. Finally one other way to give is simply through donating your quality used goods. If you have something that might be of value to someone else and you aren't using it, why not share it? Clothes are one of the first things that come to mind and are an easy way to get into the spirit of giving.

Whichever way you choose to be of service, it doesn't matter. Just do it! Sharing your time can offer you perspective on how blessed you truly are. I know it makes me feel that way. There simply is no reason not to give. You will feel better, you will be helping others, you will be doing the right thing, you will be strengthening your foundation and you will be making a positive impact in your community and the world.

> *If you want happiness for an hour, take a nap.*
> *If you want happiness for a day, go fishing.*
> *If you want happiness for a year, inherit a fortune.*
> *If you want happiness for a lifetime, help somebody.*
>
> **—Chinese Proverb**

Moments of Clarity

What are some ways that you could be of service?

What are some ways that you have been of service in the past?

CHAPTER 30

Get Curious

cur·i·ous

adjective: **curious**

1. eager to learn or know; inquisitive.
   "They were **curious** *about the new store that opened."*

Are you in a bit of a rut? Feeling like you are going through the motions
day after day? Feeling like there is more to life than what it is currently offering
you? Get curious and try something new. We aren't meant to be stagnant. We
were put here to learn, be fluid, and grow. The world is your oyster. Seriously. Step
out of your routine. Expand your horizons. The more you try the more alive you
will feel. Take a chance and set aside your fears.

Looking back to my childhood, I feel fortunate that I had an enterprising yet
slightly quirky spirit, which laid the groundwork for my work and continues
to flow through me today. Growing up I loved baseball and its rich history. I
collected antique baseball cards and could name any number of facts had you
asked me. One day I came across a magazine that had the addresses of a bunch of
retired legends of the game. This was back in the mid-late 1970s and was before
autograph collecting became big business. I decided to write to all of these guys.
I made out a list with the date of when I sent the self-addressed stamped letter
and also recorded when and if I received it back. Each day had the potential for
me to be like Christmas when I walked out to the mailbox hoping to find some
treasured autographed index card in the returned envelopes. Some of the guys
would add an extra card or a personal letter and it was quite exciting for this little
boy from Salem, Oregon to be receiving notes and autographs from the likes of
Satchel Paige, Hank Aaron, Stan Musial and Duke Snider just to name a few. I
remember Don Newcomb set the record for getting back to me in only eight days.
I think Hank Aaron was the longest at just over a year.

The point I am trying to make is, you can create your own fun and spice things
up by trying something new. The sky's the limit. I feel extremely blessed that I
have had a curious and adventurous spirit. It seems like I have spent my whole
life searching out wonder and trying something new. I just assume the Universe
will always say yes to what I set my heart and mind on, even when I am scared
initially. It didn't matter if it was entering and completing an Ironman triathlon,

leaving my family business, creating my own short films, setting up my own book tour, writing children's books, moving to LA or combining my love of history and cycling by riding my bicycle across the United States. I just wanted to play in areas that were new to me and that I felt drawn to explore. I had to satisfy my ever-growing curious nature and give myself the freedom to learn about myself and expand who I was becoming.

There are so many ways to get curious and try something new. You could go big like I did or you could make it as simple as taking in an exhibit at your local museum or eating at a new restaurant. You could try a new hairstyle. How about taking a class that interests you at the local community college? How about picking up a new sport? Go write a book, we all have a story to tell. The possibilities are endless but you have to take action. Just like I did when I was a little kid by writing those baseball players. Allow your curiosity to flourish and feel alive in ways you never thought possible!

Moments of Clarity

What are some things that you are curious about?

What are some things that you have wanted to try yet felt fear for one reason or another?

How would you feel if you stepped into your fear to accomplish this goal?

CHAPTER 31

Let Go of Control

con·trol

verb: **control**

1. to exercise restraint or direction over; dominate; command.

   "She did her best to **control** *her anger over the mistake."*

Anxiety is quite prevalent in our world today and I believe holds so many of us back. So much of our anxiety comes from trying to control every aspect of our lives. I know, because I used to be the king of trying to control things. But as I began to release my tight hold and started to allow things to settle and happen on their own accord, I found a beauty in the release, a sense of calm and ease take over. We are not meant to hold onto things as tightly as we do.

Letting go of control is just as important as taking control. If you hold onto anything too tightly it will be smothered and suffocate. Same thing applies to our life, work and goals. You have to leave some room for things to breath. You have to leave some room for those synchronistic events and chance meetings that come about when you are in alignment and trusting the process. Living our lives authentically requires trust. There really is no such thing as security or even control. We make our plans and try to do the best that we can, but ultimately we don't know what tomorrow is going to bring.

There truly is something beautiful about letting go of control. First of all, we are acknowledging trust in the process and a higher power and secondly it removes most of the weight that we carry trying to control everything in the first place. Why wouldn't you want to go through life feeling lighter? I am not saying to work any less hard, but what I am saying is, do your work in an inspired, smarter way, enjoy the process and then let it go and see what happens. There is absolutely no gain to be made from worrying with an overactive mind. It just creates a negative mindset that will ultimately hold you back as you become bitter.

How do we trust enough to let go of control and surrender when we are feeling anxious and holding tight? For me it was the fact that I had become so unhappy in my life trying to control every aspect of it especially in regard to my career. I figured that I had nothing to lose and I wanted to try and find peace of mind and a true happiness. To trust and let go of control was the first step. I know it's not easy, but I can assure you it is worth it. It's an incredibly important part of building a successful foundation.

I had a realization a few years back while on an airplane about how much I used to try and control all aspects of my life. I wasn't always a nervous flyer, but as I got older I found myself becoming more and more anxious. It became something that I really didn't look forward to doing. While sitting on a plane, my time was mine but it wasn't if that makes sense. I would feel that I was being held captive. Of course I wasn't literally being held captive, but I was being held captive by my own desire and need to control everything in my life including the flights that I had absolutely no control of whatsoever. It got to the point that I would get a vodka soda as soon the beverage cart came by to calm my nerves even though I am not much of a drinker. I would then put in my ear buds, listen to some calming music and try to meditate by doing deep breathing exercises while praying there was no turbulence. But for some reason this particular flight was different. All of a sudden while sitting there just before takeoff, I found myself hyper aware of the need to surrender control and just be. Surprisingly I was able to do this. It's like I had no choice. The proverbial weight just lifted off of me and I was at peace. I felt transfixed. I spent most of the flight looking out the window at the clouds in a truly relaxed state. Normally I would just sit there feeling anxious and lost because I wasn't in control. But this was different. I had then realized how tired I had become while trying to control every aspect of my life.

It felt so good giving up control of this; it made me want to feel this way all of the time. Total surrender, total peace, total acceptance of the real me; the person who sometimes struggles and who isn't always fearless. Not the person that I would trick myself into believing I was; the super hero that was always in control that should be producing, creating, succeeding and advancing ALL THE TIME.

This powerful sense of surrender that came over me on the plane showed that there was nothing that needed to be fixed, I was always whole. I knew that my life wasn't sustainable anymore in my old way of thinking and needing to be so tightly in control. It had left me tired, unfulfilled, and with a false sense of identity. To free myself, I just needed to let go. I want you to feel free as well.

Moments of Clarity

Where are some areas of your life that you might be too controlling?

How could you do a better job of letting go of control?

CHAPTER 32

Go for a Walk

walk

verb: **walk**

1. to move about or travel on foot for exercise or pleasure.
   *"We can **walk** in the park after lunch."*

Want to get your head clear about something? Want to refill your cup?
Want to get your creative juices flowing? Want to change your attitude? Want to
give your body a little exercise? Want to relieve some stress? Want to spend a few
minutes visualizing your dream or goal? Want to spend some time being truly
present? Want to connect with a friend? Go take a walk!

Walking is such a powerful cure-all and it's free. I can't tell you how many times
I have gone for a walk and felt totally rejuvenated during and after. It's a fantastic
way to get unstuck and wake your senses back up.

I absolutely love to walk. Looking back at all of the different places that I have
lived, one of the first things I did when I arrived was to find a place that I could go
walk or hike that felt peaceful to me. Some of my personal favorites were Minto-
Brown Island Park in Salem, Oregon; Lake Tahoe Rim Trail on top Mt. Rose
outside of Reno, Nevada; and Griffith Park in Los Angeles. Not only was I getting
some exercise, but I was also coming up with lots of creative ideas while out doing
it. I even practiced my TEDx presentation while hiking. Moving my body and
being out in nature really helped me internalize, memorize and be totally present
with it.

While out walking I love how everything slows down. I pay attention to the
flowers, trees and everything else I come across. It's a great way to practice
the art of being present. It's also a great way to continue to introduce beauty
and gratitude on a daily basis. Taking a moment for myself while out hiking or
walking has always been medicine for my soul and an incredibly important tool
for my growth process. I encourage you to make it part of yours as well. Go for
a walk.

Moments of Clarity

Are there some areas near where you live that you could go walk?

CHAPTER 33

Do What You Love

do

verb: **do**

1. to perform (an act, duty, role, etc.)
2. to accomplish; finish; complete.
    "Just **do** *it one step at a time."*

Do what you love. It is as simple as it sounds. How many of you do things just because you think you should? Or maybe because something once served you but is no longer needed yet became a habit? Or possibly because someone suggested you do it, but it didn't really register with you? I think all of us can relate to one or more of these. How we find ourselves in these situations can vary and there are as many reasons as there are people out in the world. Let's use work for starters. Maybe you took a job out of necessity and then became complacent at it or stayed because you felt you had to. Maybe you hopped right into a particular job market out of college because you thought you were expected to. Or maybe you felt familial pressure to carry on the family business even though it didn't inspire you. All of these situations could find a person not doing what they love. More than likely you found yourself in a state of going through the motions and not truly enjoying life because you were in a situation that either never served you or doesn't serve you anymore. I can relate. I have been there too. That is why I eventually left my family business after eleven years. I felt that I had stopped growing and knew in my heart I was supposed to do something different. Although I didn't know it at the time, I needed to learn, grow and express myself through books, acting and speaking. I didn't realize it was inside of me until I left. I just knew I had to take that first step of leaving. Since then I have felt happier, more fulfilled, and share a true excitement about my purpose.

It is very important that you be able to do the things that you love and enjoy so that you can truly feel the full capacity of who you are and what you are about. You deserve to live life on your own terms. And please remember, it's ok to start small. I understand that most people can't just go and quite their current job. It is possible though to start looking around for others or maybe take some classes on the side to begin to develop some new skills that might lead to a new opportunity in doing something that you enjoy more. The important thing is to get some momentum going and clarity flowing. If you love to write and want to make it your profession maybe take a creative writing class or work part-time doing something you love until you can do it full time. If there's a will there's a way to make it happen.

I want to share a story with you that I found very inspiring about someone who did just that. In 2018, a man named Phil Coyne retired from his job as an usher for the Pittsburgh Pirates major league baseball team. Initially, there is nothing terribly noteworthy about that, but when you find out that Phil is ninety-nine years old and had been doing that job for eighty-one years and over six thousand games, it's truly incredible. I love baseball and it's colorful history. So Phil's story resonates with me even more. It's hard for me to wrap my head around the fact that Phil started working for the Pirates at the age of eighteen in 1936…1936! To put that into perspective, Lou Gehrig was still the first baseman for the New Yankees and our country was in the middle of *The Great Depression*. I can only imagine all that Phil witnessed on the job. Talk about doing something you love! Phil is the total embodiment of that. Might we all be so lucky to do something that we love for half of that time! Do what you love. Just like Phil.

Moments of Clarity

What do you truly love to do?

Are you allowing yourself to do it?

What can you do, right now, to be able to do, or get close to doing what you love?

CHAPTER 34

Visualize

vis·u·al·ize

verb: **visualize**

1. to recall or form mental images or pictures.

   "She enjoyed making vision boards to **visualize** *her future."*

I would imagine that some of you might be familiar with the law of attraction. The law of attraction basically states that thoughts are things; what we put our attention to will expand; whatever we put our focus on will become reality. It is the belief that by focusing on positive or negative thoughts people can bring positive or negative experiences into their life. The belief is based on the idea that everything is energy that carries a vibration. Ourselves included. And through the process of "like energy attracts like energy" a person can and will attract what their mind is focused on depending on the vibration of energy they are holding. So by staying mindful, holding a higher vibration and creating positive habits of visualization, we can focus on ways to improve our lives.

The process of visualization is similar. To be able to create the life that we want it helps if we can imagine what that life will look like, even right down to the smallest details. It can be as simple as creating a picture in your mind. Remember as a child when you might have imagined being a fireman or ballerina? You may have even gone so far as to act out those dreams with your friends. Visualizing the successful completion of a goal is really no different from what we did as children when we played make believe. What dreams or goals do you aspire to? Do you want a more fulfilling job? Would you like a healthy, loving relationship? Would you like to author that book that you have always wanted to write? Do you want to train for and finish a marathon? All of these goals are open to visualization on your part.

You can visualize while lying down before going to sleep or as you are waking up. You could do it while exercising. You can visualize while sitting down as you take a break from work. You could do it while taking a shower or a bath. I used to visualize a lot while out walking or hiking. Visualization has played such an important role in my life in helping me realize many of my goals and dreams as well as helps me strengthen my foundation. I encourage you to make it a part of your life as well. I want you to manifest your heart's desire!

One of the experiences that really stood out for me was while I was preparing for the 2005 Vineman Ironman triathlon. It had been fifteen years since I last completed an Ironman, but I knew in my heart that I wanted to finish another one with my then eleven-year-old son watching who had yet to be born when I raced previously. I wanted to be able to surprise him and have him run the last one hundred yards and cross the finish line with me and share the magic of the experience. So what did I do? While training and preparing for this race months in advance, I kept playing the scene over and over in my head of my son and I crossing the finish line together. I would visualize the two of us laughing and smiling, crossing the finish line while swimming at 5:30 in the morning. I would see us finishing together while on long training rides. I would imagine us finishing together while I was running in the rain. I held that thought all of the time. It was very powerful for me. I would often become emotional while thinking about it. And let me tell you that feeling emotional is powerful when visualizing. It means that your visualization and energetic vibrations are really working together with what you want to accomplish. When I would "see" him finishing the race with me, I was able to tap into how special the moment would feel. I had that passion and emotion from my two previous experiences. I wanted my son and I to have that experience together.

Come race morning I had my usual bout of jitters and nervousness, but I also had a great sense of calm. My son and his mother were with me, and I felt like I had a special mission that day. This race wasn't just about me; it was for both of us.

It was a long day, but I was motivated the entire time. Everything went perfectly. My body held up, my son got to see me "in action," and I was able to fulfill my dream of having him cross the finish line with me! It happened just the way I had visualized it all those months before. As I came out of the black night into the lit up finishing area, I saw him standing there with a big smile on his face. He had been so patient the entire fourteen hours that I was out racing and it made me feel so happy to be able to share this moment with him. As he stuck his hand out to give me a high five I held onto it and started pulling him along with me. It definitely surprised him. And as we made it toward the finish banner, I had such a feeling of pride and pure joy. It was a very special experience to say the least and one of the best days of my life.

I want to share another brief story with you on how I used visualization in a different way. This time I utilized it to help me move through a very stressful experience. I was working as a counselor at a boy's treatment ranch in Northern California in 1996. On occasion it could turn into a rough place. Unfortunately most of the boys had been abused one way or another during their lives and didn't have a good foundation of being loved, accepted and having boundaries set for them. Because of this, there was a lot of anger and other inappropriate behavior. Sometimes we had to break up fights or were actually attacked ourselves physically as well as verbally. It wasn't an easy two years of employment, but I truly wanted to make a difference and positively reach some of the kids so that they could have a better finish than their start.

One day I remember having to break up a fight between two boys with some of my co-workers. After a fight we would usually take the offending parties to separate rooms where they could cool down and become "safe" again. Due to California law, we weren't able to lock these rooms, so one of the staff had to hold the door shut from the outside and watch through a window to make sure that the boy was being safe toward himself. Many times while this happened, the offending boy would still be "fired up" from his fight and would take it out on staff verbally. It also wasn't unusual for a troubled teen to spit on the window or try to urinate underneath the small crack at the base of the door to try and get some on us. Well after this one particular fight, the boy that I was watching was really letting me have it verbally with all kinds of offensive words and threats. Now I knew what he was saying wasn't really about me. He was basically scared, hurting inside and wanting attention. Believe me, it is really hard not to feel for these kids, but when you are getting barraged with negativity, it's also hard to not to let some of it slip into your consciousness. After a while I was getting really worn out from listening to his angry rants and threats. So to counter what was happening, I decided to come up with a mantra right then, that I continue to use to this day. I began to say to myself, "I am love, I spread love and I am surrounded by love." I just kept repeating it over and over in my head. It was amazing how it began to help me almost immediately. And after a few minutes you know what? The young man began to relax as well. Whether or not it was coincidence or he actually felt my energy change, it doesn't matter. What matters is that I was able to find comfort, love and relaxation during a very stressful experience.

I want you to try an exercise. Make a list of what you would like to see come into your life. Be very specific with it. By very specific, I mean include all the details of what you visualize for your future. If you want a new job, don't simply write, "I want a new job." Write the kind of job you want. What kind of people you want to work with. What your hours and pay structure will be. That same specificity applies to everything on your list. After you've written your list visualize yourself in those situations. Imagine being in that new job, on that dream vacation, or crossing the finish line of a marathon! Play those movies over in your head where you are the star of the show making all of your dreams come true. Have fun with it. It will also really lift your spirits. Visualization is such a powerful tool. I encourage you to make it a habit in your life.

Moments of Clarity

How might you be able to incorporate visualization into your life?

What would you like to visualize to fruition?

CHAPTER 35

Be Easy on Yourself

ea·sy

adjective: **easy**
1. free from pain, discomfort, worry, or care.
2. providing or conducive to ease or comfort; comfortable.
   *"He was very good at taking it **easy** on himself."*

How many of you actually listen to yourself talk? I bet if you paid
attention to the things you say to yourself about yourself you would be amazed!
Every time you say something negative, you are planting a negative seed. What
happens is simple: you will begin to live out what you tell yourself: "I can't do
this, I'm an idiot, I am a fool for thinking that," etc. The more you plant these
negative seeds, the harder it will become. Try to become aware of how you
communicate with yourself and others. Just imagine how you would feel and
what you could accomplish, if you surround yourself with positive and life
affirming statements and visions. It really does make a difference. To tap into the
best versions of ourselves, we have to clear out our negative patterns and beliefs.

> *What you say to yourself will seal your fate*
> *Whether it's thoughts of love or words of hate*
> *You map your course, no matter which route you choose*
> *So pick quite wisely, you have everything to lose*

—G. Brian Benson *(stanza from poem "Keys to Life")*

Negative self-talk is just one way that you can be hard on yourself. Another is to
hold extremely high expectations of perfection. I can relate to this one personally.
There has been many times where I have spent a lot of anxious energy being
worried about having something come out just "perfect." That's not to say you
shouldn't do the best job you possibly can. Of course give it your best. However,
if we hold on too tightly to perfection our creativity becomes stifled and we are
never able to truly enjoy the process. For some, the pressure of having something
be perfect, keeps them from even starting. And for others, it never allows them

to finish because it will never be "perfect." Please don't be that person. Just go for it! And if you make a mistake or fail, keep trying. Cut yourself some slack if you make a mistake. It's going to happen. We all make mistakes. It's part of life. We are constantly learning and growing and part of that equation is to make mistakes from time to time.

My own come-to-awareness moment was the week after I released my first children's book, *Steve the Alien,* a few years back. I was extremely proud of birthing this book and it even hit number one on Amazon the day of its launch. I worked my butt off in so many ways. Not only with the launch, but with the self-production of the book, guiding and directing my talented illustrator, Paul Hernandez, and repeatedly having to deal with a variety of issues along the way. But after it came out, I found myself really depressed. And I stayed this way for almost a week. Normally you would think someone would be ecstatic about creating a successful book, and parts of me were, however something was missing. Looking back, part of my unhappiness stemmed from my own lofty expectations of how the book would do. Talk about not being easy on myself! It had only been out a week and it hit the top ranking in it's category during the launch, what more could I expect? More importantly, I also realized a number-one book wasn't enough to make me a happy person. I will always be working on that from the inside out. Instead of patting myself on the back and celebrating for a job well done, I felt like I didn't want to do this anymore. I was tired. I was tired of pushing, striving and putting so much pressure on myself. At the end of that week I told myself that I wasn't going to do this anymore if it wasn't going to bring me joy and happiness. That was the proverbial "straw that broke the camel's back" for me.

Since then, I have been quite conscious of simply being joyful and present during the process and then taking pride in the finished product. I was putting so much pressure on myself to have a hit book or film that I realized it was just another way for me to try and look outside of myself for the happiness and love that I needed to have come from within. I think we all have a tendency to do this in one way or another. Be easy on yourself no matter the situation. Whether it relates to a job, relationship or a creative project that you are undertaking. Once I really internalized that, things began to change for me.

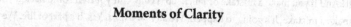

Moments of Clarity

How do you treat yourself?

Do you treat yourself with the same kindness and support you show others?

What are you trying to prove and why? Questions to ponder.

CHAPTER 36

Laugh

laugh

verb: **laugh**

1. to find amusement or pleasure in something.
2. to show emotion (such as mirth, joy, or scorn) with a chuckle or explosive vocal sound.
   *"They had a great **laugh** while watching the comic perform."*

Have you ever had one of those days where nothing seemed to be going right and then all of a sudden you saw or heard something really funny that just totally turned your attitude around because you started to laugh? I'm sure we all have. I know it's cliché' but laughter really is the best medicine.

To laugh is to feel alive. To laugh with another is to be spiritually connected with them. Laughter brings hope. Laughter brings relief. Laughter heals our bodies. Laughter brings people together. Why would anyone not want to laugh? I think the best way to have a laugh is to share it with another person.

Luckily for us, there are plenty of wonderful places to search out a laugh if we need one: TV, movies, the Internet, books, magazines, politics, friends and life experiences. And let's all start by laughing at ourselves more. Why aren't we doing that? Everyone has become so serious and easily offended these days. Let's turn down the ego and turn up the "loosen up." I remember when I was on a trip to Europe with my good friend Jordan and some members of his family. We were eating at a really nice restaurant in Frankfurt, Germany and as we were leaving the maître' d was shaking everyone's hand goodbye. Well, I didn't notice that he was standing at the top of a small set of stairs. So as I made eye contact with him and shook his hand I then tripped and fell flat on my face below everyone. Being the goofy guy that I can be at times, I immediately stood up and yelled, "Safe!" Just like I had just slid across home plate. They all got a good laugh out of that and it took some of the sting out of my embarrassment for falling down. Jordan and I still laugh about that to this day!

Life is funny. People are funny. Try to look for and find humor in everything you do and everywhere you go. It makes life so much more fun and interesting, not to mention the quality of your life will instantly improve and your foundation will be solidified. What are you waiting for? Laughter is instant sunshine.

Moments of Clarity

What makes you laugh?

How could you include more laughter in your life?

CHAPTER 37

Create an Intention

in·ten·tion

noun: **intention**

1. purpose or attitude toward the effect of one's actions or conduct.
2. what one intends to do or bring about.
   *"She announced her **intention** to look for another job."*

Through the years, I have been blessed to have set and accomplished a number of goals of mine, but as I get older, and a little bit wiser, I have learned that there is an even more powerful tool we have at our disposal. It is called an intention; and I really like to hold intentions. For me they feel broader and have a wider base to sit upon. Goals are great. But sometimes they can feel narrow in regard to the process of how we are going to get there to achieve them. But with an intention, the sky's the limit in regard to the path that will take us there. Let me give you an example. Remember when I had mentioned earlier that when I was really little, I told my Mom that I was put here to inspire people? After I left my family business and unexpectedly wrote my first self-help book, I felt like I had just boarded that train to "inspiring" people and my ticket to do that was via books. So that became my goal. But what I didn't realize then was that writing books was just going to be one of many ways to create positive content. As I began to work on my own self-growth process, I had the opportunity to try some other things, like acting and speaking. And as I kept my mind open, I began to create some unique and inspiring projects via other forms of media. What I realized is that by being open to these other ways of creating, I was still on my original path of inspiring others but it didn't just have to be through books. By having that seed planted and holding the original intention of being put here to "inspire people," I was introduced to a lot of fun, exciting and empowering experiences that I had no idea were inside of me that still had an opportunity to make a big difference. Keep an open mind as you set your goals and intentions; you never know where they may lead or the path that they will take you on. Happily expect the unexpected!

Moments of Clarity

What are some intentions that you currently have?

What are some intentions that you could set for yourself?

LIGHT BULB MOMENTS

Be True to Yourself

The single greatest wisdom I think I've ever received is that the key to fulfillment, success, happiness, and contentment in life is when you align your personality with what your soul actually came to do.

—Oprah Winfrey

You've got to express yourself in life, and it's better out than in. What you reveal, you heal.

—Chris Martin

To help yourself, you must be yourself. Be the best that you can be. When you make a mistake, learn from it, pick yourself up and move on.

—Dave Pelzer

To be yourself in a world that is constantly trying to make you something else is the greatest accomplishment

—Ralph Waldo Emerson

To be beautiful means to be yourself. You don't need to be accepted by others. You need to accept yourself.

—Bindi Irwin

If you celebrate your differentness, the world will, too. It believes exactly what you tell it through the words you use to describe yourself, the actions you take to care for yourself, and the choices you make to express yourself. Tell the world you are a one-

of-a-kind creation who came here to experience wonder and spread joy. Expect to be accommodated.

—Victoria Moran

We are all here to learn about ourselves and inspire others in our own unique way.

—G. Brian Benson

Who were you before the world told you what you were not?

—Bryant McGill

The essential lesson I've learned in life is to just be yourself. Treasure the magnificent being that you are and recognize first and foremost you're not here as a human being only. You're a spiritual being having a human experience.

—Wayne Dyer

Be who you are and say what you feel, because those who mind don't matter and those who matter don't mind.

—Dr. Seuss

Courage starts with showing up and letting ourselves be seen. Because true belonging only happens when we present our authentic, imperfect selves to the world, our sense of belonging can never be greater than our level of self-acceptance.

—Brené Brown

CHAPTER 38

Allow Yourself to Feel

feel

verb: **feel**

1. to be emotionally affected by.
2. to have a sensation of (something), other than by sight, hearing, taste, or smell.
   *"He **felt** the beauty of the Northern Lights sink into his being."*

Allowing ourselves to feel is an important part of building and strengthening our foundations. It is imperative that we "feel" our feelings. When we start to feel feelings instead of pushing them away we begin to heal. We also begin to feel better, have fewer relationship and health problems and experience less stress. We are also able to communicate better, have sharper focus and lead healthier lives. It all starts with a willingness to experience our emotions to the fullest. Feelings are very similar to ocean waves. They start by building, eventually peak and then dissipate. When we are able to feel an emotion all of the way, it has no reason to hang around and will eventually begin to have less of an impact on us.

One Saturday morning while driving my car through surprisingly light LA traffic on my way to a favorite hiking destination, I stopped at a red light. My head was a bit sleepy and my thoughts mellow as I innocently began my day. Seemingly out of nowhere came an extremely loud crash, which brought my attention front and center as I then noticed a car heading right for me spinning out of control having been t-boned by another one. My natural reaction was to duck down as glass and small debris rained down as the car narrowly missed mine by inches. It seemed to be over as quickly as it started. Then things got even more interesting.

Although it's cliché to say that "life is short and that we should fully embrace it because tomorrow isn't a guarantee," it can be really easy to overlook that fact as we lead our busy lives. My experience that morning provided a stark reminder that as cliché as the "life is short" statement is, it's 110 percent true and things

CAN change in an instant. That is why it's so important to truly love and enjoy every moment that we can. And sometimes we need an experience to really shake us up to point us back to the what's really important. I wonder if that was the case for the two drivers involved in the crash. I also wondered if this was a wake-up call for either of them to make changes in their lives. I certainly know that I have had my fair share through the years.

When I got out of my car to see if both drivers were ok, I began to *feel*. I felt their fear, I felt their anxiety and I felt their mortality. I also felt totally alive. By bearing witness to and almost being a part of their potentially tragic accident I began to feel at a much deeper level. Over the course of the next thirty minutes as emergency responders came and statements were given I felt very connected to humanity. As spiritual beings having a raw human experience in truth we are always connected, yet sometimes it takes a traumatic experience for us to really get out of our mind/ego state to let down our shields and allow that connection to flow through. I felt a lot of compassion for both drivers and was quite relieved that they were all right.

I am truly sorry that there was an accident but I give thanks that I found myself sitting at the red light that lazy Saturday morning. I was given an opportunity to be a helpful, calming influence for the drivers. And because I found myself in that situation, it reminded me of the value and importance to be present and awake in my body, to truly feel my feelings and to be reminded of the connection that we all share.

Awake

Awake my mind, you bittersweet tool
Which leads one true or to play the fool
Weakened thoughts grasp, away from the core
Leave me tired, hungry, wanting more

Awake my heart and step into love
Melt away young scars and rise above
Confusions kiss, led me astray

I turn within to mute the grey

Awake my truth, thy grand unmasked self
Hidden, buried, found; authentic wealth
Our life's purpose, comfort, joy and ease
Guidance from within, eager to please

Awake my spirit, fears set aside
Soul's perfection, fervent, loving guide
Flowing love, our birthright, path, desire
Flame burns bright from this heavenly fire

Awake myself to all I can be
Uncluttered vision resides in me
Potential and greatness that is I
There are no limits under the sky

Awake myself to my truthful worth
Love, light, perfection; peace, joy and mirth
Creative fire; gifts deep inside all
Intuition beckons, I heed its call

Awake my energy, guiding spark
Send me soaring; to purpose, on mark
Alert, alive to all that can be
Seeking, shining; as far as I see

—G. Brian Benson

Moments of Clarity

Do you allow yourself to feel?

How do you handle it when feelings start to come up?

CHAPTER 39

Learn at Your Own Pace

pace

noun: **pace**
1. a rate of activity, progress, growth, performance, etc.
2. a rate of movement.
   *"The **pace** of the course suited everyone's unique learning styles."*

We are all unique. There isn't another one of us in the Universe. We all learn and assimilate information differently. How you learn is different from how I learn. How you are reading and understanding this sentence could be vastly different from how I read this sentence. We have similarities and differences and finding common ground may take a different kind of communication. I know that I am more of a kinetic and visual learner; meaning that I retain what I am learning much stronger if I am able to read or be hands-on during the learning process. Workshops and seminars have always been tough for me because a lot of times when I was just sitting there and listening things seemed to go in one ear and out the other. I have trouble focusing and it is harder for me to retain what I am hearing. Before I realized which ways of learning suited me, I often became frustrated with myself or others became frustrated with me because I wasn't able to retain what they were trying to teach me. I wish I knew in high school and college what I know now. I may have been able to utilize a kinetic or visual style of learning, which would have helped me out tremendously. I wonder how many kids sitting in classrooms today are struggling because they aren't being taught in a way that suits their individual needs. Dyslexia and autism are just a few issues that people may be dealing with that require special attention while learning. We all learn differently and at our own pace. And that's ok!

I recently received a message on my YouTube channel from someone who watched my black and white short film "Searching for Happiness." I love receiving comments from people who enjoy the messages I am conveying in my films and videos but this one left me feeling really touched. It empathetically opened up my heart and made me truly realize that we aren't all playing with the same hand. I am going to change the name of the person for their privacy and share our messages with you verbatim so you can fully understand what I am talking about and experience the beauty in their vulnerability and the struggle with their learning issue.

Susan: "Okay, here goes nothing: I'm autistic and I find myself completely in the dark as to what story is being told. [I am] unable to read behavior in people without dialogue. And it frustrates me immensely that I don't get it, because it's so obvious to everybody else. Would somebody explain? Please?"

My response: "Hi Susan...thank you for the kind words about it being visually stunning and for the music. I appreciate that. To answer your question, basically the main character is unhappy. He is unsure why and is desperately trying to figure out why. He is even reading about how to become happy (in a book) but it isn't helping him. So throughout the film he witnesses random acts of kindness by others. And as they happen, those involved colorize. It's just another way to make the point that those who interact with and help others can find an authentic version of happiness. So at the end when the main character kind of by accident returns the ring to the woman who dropped it, he finally understands that to find happiness one needs to connect with and lend a hand when we can. So he then colorizes as well as he understands that. Does that help? I hope. Feel free to ask more questions if you need to. Thank you for watching our film. Sincerely, Brian"

Susan: "G. Brian Benson, thank you so much for taking the time to explain. I watched it again and now it's even more stunning. And 'wow' sums it up nicely. Thank you so much for explaining. It's often said autists lack empathy but that's not true; we do understand. And it's through your explanation that I was able to emotionally connect to the characters. And, the film being what it is, I think you may understand what your explanation means to me, what it has done for me: helping me connect to others. And to see the message of the film reflected in your actions...I struggle with finding the right words but things like admiration, respect, and hope tumble through my mind. Thank you for explaining and thanks to all involved for making this film, thank you so much."

I realize that if you haven't watched the short film (on YouTube and my website) that it might be a bit confusing for you, but the whole point I am trying to make is that Susan's ability to learn is different than most of our abilities to learn. And it has nothing to do with her intellect, but her wiring. She's obviously a very intelligent person but needed some guidance to understand the movie because there is no dialogue and she wasn't able to read the expressions of the characters because that is not how her brain works.

Be open to the differences of others to find the common ground of learning and experiencing life together. And please be easy on yourself. Learn at your own pace. Figure out what is the best way for you to thrive and utilize it. Once we can begin to figure out our strengths and eliminate our weaknesses through self-awareness our foundation is sure to become stronger.

Moments of Clarity

Do you know if you are an auditory, kinetic or visual learner? Or possibly a combination of the three?

How might you benefit by knowing what type of learning style suits you best?

CHAPTER 40

Be Kind

kind

adjective: **kind**

1. of a good or benevolent nature or disposition.
2. indulgent, considerate, or helpful; humane.
   *"She had such a **kind** nature toward others."*

Wayne Dyer once said, "It's better to be kind than to be right." I agree.
Watch how everything improves when you are genuinely kind. Your attitude
improves, those around you treat you better, your experiences become richer
and even random positive stuff just seems to happen. Not only that but you feel
better about yourself, you feel better about your environment, the people around
you and what you have to work with. You will also be much more appreciative for
what you have.

Let me give you an example of how doing a simple act of kindness can go a long
ways. Living in Los Angeles and having to navigate the extremely busy freeways
and city streets, I found that this daily ritual offers a great opportunity for me
to focus on the art of giving and being kind. Each day I'm given the choice to
let people in front of me. Or not. I will tell you that when I do let someone in
to merge or to switch lanes, it makes the rest of my drive that much smoother
and more enjoyable. The actual act itself is quite simple yet it totally changes my
energy in a positive way. It makes me feel like I am contributing to life instead of
taking from it.

Conversely, it turns negative on those days when I am feeling competitive
or stubborn and don't allow someone to merge in front of me. It becomes a
competition. Why do I do that? It's not like I was going to arrive late to my
destination because I let one person in front of me on a freeway that is crawling at
a snail's pace anyways.

We are all in this crazy, beautiful life together and driving on the freeway is the
perfect metaphor for that. By helping and looking out for one another, even in
the simplest of ways, and showing an authentic kindness to each person we come
across, our own personal journey is much more fulfilling and enjoyable. And
believe me that goodness spreads like wildfire when others witness it.

So next time you're given the opportunity to let someone merge into your lane while driving, don't hesitate. You'll feel better, they will be appreciative and the positivity shared will inspire others to do the same. And of course it doesn't have to just be on the freeway, help someone out at the grocery store or hold the door when entering a building. Say hello to a stranger, make a donation to someone less fortunate, or pay a compliment to someone who looks like they could use one. Kindness is another form of beauty and an important part of your foundation. Kindness is a habit worth cultivating in your daily life. Share it, spread it and be it.

Moments of Clarity

What could you do to be more kind?

CHAPTER 41

Leave Ten Minutes Early

ear·ly

adverb: **early**

1. before the usual or appointed time; ahead of time.
2. near the beginning of a course, process, or series.
   *"They were always **early** to class."*

How often do you find yourself rushing late to work or someplace else where you need to be? How does it make you feel? Stressed? Angry? Guilty? There's a very simple technique you can use to eliminate all of those unwanted feelings that come from being rushed. Try leaving ten to fifteen minutes early. (Simple, right?)

I realize there is the occasional situation when we're running late due to reasons out of our control, but the majority of the time, it doesn't have to be that way. Why not just try heading out the door a few minutes earlier than usual? You will be amazed at how peaceful and restful your drive to work can be! If you miss a traffic light, it's no big deal. If you get stuck at a railroad crossing; same thing, no big deal! Knowing that you have a few extra minutes will help you to relax and make your commute so much smoother, easier and less stressful.

When I started leaving ten minutes early to go to work, I noticed the difference immediately. I arrived at work feeling much more peaceful and balanced. I was ready to start the day. Prior to leaving ten minutes early, I would be scrambling in to work, usually carrying a load of anxiety and stress. I would start those days feeling behind and definitely not in flow. Not a great way to start. Once I was in the habit of running early instead of running late, my stress and anxiety levels went down and I was more ready for the day. Allow yourself that extra time; you will be glad you did. If you live in Los Angeles like me, better make it forty-five minutes!

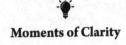

Moments of Clarity

How often are you on time?

Is being late an issue for you?

What are some ways that you could help yourself be on time?

CHAPTER 42

Write Down Your Thoughts

thought

noun: thought

1. the act or process of thinking; mental activity.
    "He enjoyed the process of sharing his **thoughts.***"*

How many times have you had something rolling around in your head that was bothering you? It's a very common occurrence and it can affect your moods, your productivity at work and even your sleep. Maybe the thing rolling around in your head was a misunderstanding you had with another person. Maybe you have a presentation coming up at your job, or a test on the horizon at school. It doesn't really matter what, just that it was keeping you from being present and centered.

My advice is to write down what is bothering you on a piece of paper or in a journal. Let it all come out. By writing down what is bothering you, you are essentially identifying your problem. By identifying your problem, you are able to release it from your mind and hopefully that will stop the nagging, sometimes debilitating, effects of what is bothering you. I realize it doesn't necessarily solve what you are dealing with, but by confronting and identifying it; you are putting it front and center and accepting it. This can be a big relief to your mental makeup. Let the piece of paper deal with the worry. This will enable you to manage the problem at the appropriate time, and not continue to have to carry the heaviness that you had been feeling. You could make it a daily occurrence (almost like journaling) or you could just write down your thoughts whenever you feel the need to; when you know you have an issue holding you back. It's well worth it, and allows you to connect to the deeper part of yourself. A part of yourself that often knows *exactly* what you need.

I am a big list maker. Writing down my to-do list might not be as cathartic as writing down an issue I am having or journaling, but it does free up my mind in the same way so that I don't have to carry around the worry of forgetting what it is that I need to do. Worry can be such an energy drain. Why not spend your energy on other things like having fun and being curious and creative? Sounds good to me.

Moments of Clarity

Do you keep a daily journal?

How could you benefit by writing down your thoughts?

CHAPTER 43

Attitude of Gratitude

gra·ti·tude

noun: gratitude

1. the quality or feeling of being grateful or thankful.
   "She had a lot of **gratitude** *for her friends."*

Our attitude is the lens through which we see the world. That's a pretty powerful statement isn't it? It's true. The thoughts that we emit and the way that we convey those thoughts determine the experience that we are going to have in life.

I would like you to close your eyes and take a deep breath. As you let your breath out slowly, think about all the things in your life for which you are thankful. It can be anything, big or small. Your family, your bicycle, the country you live in, time spent with friends, your favorite pair of shoes, and the flowers in your garden are all great examples. Giving thanks for what we have may be one of the single most important things we can do for ourselves. It puts us in a positive frame of mind, helps us see the good in all things and lets others know we are open to receiving more.

I realize there are some people who might feel like they don't have a lot to be thankful for. That is understandable considering what may be going on in their life at the moment. However, I believe everyone has blessings in their lives. It is very important to tap into what we are thankful for even in those darkest of days to create momentum to move forward and get to that place of gratitude. Our thoughts are very important. If you don't feel you have much to be grateful for, then that is the reality you will sit with, because you are literally telling yourself that you aren't worthy of anything better. And that is simply not true.

Try and give thanks for *all* that comes your way, the good and the bad. You may ask, "Why would I want to give thanks for something bad that happened?" Well, we are here to learn and grow, and the greatest learning opportunities usually occur during trying experiences (what a great place to hide lessons, huh?). Be thankful for them, and the new and hopefully wiser you who came out of a tough situation. The trying times will eventually pass, and you will be better prepared the next time they come around, or even better yet, you can help someone else going through a tough time with your experience.

I try and stay on top of this as much as I can, because I have down days just like everyone else. I like to give thanks when I start my day in the morning just as I am getting out of bed as well as later in the day when I am on my daily walk. I keep it simple and just go over in my head all of the things in my life that I am thankful for. It can include family and friends, material objects (clothes, car, computer, etc.), opportunities that I have had or that might be coming my way as well as simple things such as the flowers or trees that I am walking by. It can include anything and everything, past, present or future. Be creative and make it fun.

Giving thanks on a regular basis is a habit that has transformed my attitude and allows a more positive flow of experiences to come into my life, not to mention strengthened my foundation. Attitude is quite literally—everything. I want the lens that you see the world through to be kind, loving and generous.

Moments of Clarity

What are you thankful for?

I would like to challenge you to write down five to ten things a day that you are grateful for every morning. Watch your spirit lift!

CHAPTER 44

Go Within

wi·thin

adverb: **within**

1. in one's inner thought, disposition, or character.
2. in or into the interior or inner part; inside.
   "Spending time in nature allowed him to get quiet and go
   within.*"*

To go within means to turn off all exterior chatter, all pursuit of external happiness, all command of the mind/ego and control, judgment and fear. To go within is to trust a higher power and surrender to its teaching. According to writer Gary Zukav, "When we look inward, not outward, we can dismantle the parts of our personalities that have controlled us for so long—such as anger, jealousy, vindictiveness, superiority, inferiority."

We are taught to believe that happiness lies outside of us. It's not hard to see why. There are so many things to draw away our attention and provide us temporary satisfaction. It's only when we turn inward that we discover that the source of enduring fulfillment is within us.

I know that mindfulness has helped me succeed in almost every aspect of my life. By focusing regularly to go inward and take stock of where I am at it, it has allowed me to be in a more balanced flow and stay connected to the source of my thoughts, which in turn allows me to live more proactively, focused and with intention. It has also helped me immeasurably when I've struggled with a difficult decision or a personal challenge in my life.

I initially learned to trust going deep within myself during a twenty-three-day Outward Bound course when I was struggling with some personal challenges in my life. The course was in the Collegiate Peaks Mountain range just outside of Leadville, Colorado at 12,000 feet and without any modern conveniences. There were eight participants as well as two guides that challenged us, taught us new skills and new ways to think every step of the way. I had hoped to find the clarity I so desperately needed among the trees and mountain air.

I felt like a newborn baby each day as I crawled out from my warm, comfortable sleeping bag into the cold, unfamiliar mountain temperatures. One of the first things my group did at the start of the course was to climb Mt. Massive at 14,421 feet. We rock climbed, summited more 14,000 foot peaks, got used to eating beans and macaroni and cheese, splash-bathed in ice cold streams and put a lot of miles behind us hiking.

I remember feeling an entire spectrum of emotions throughout the trip (joy, bliss, confidence, confusion, anger, sadness, grief) and even surprised myself with some extensive sobbing that seemed to come from deep within me.

The highlight for me came during a three-day solo. The eight of us were spread out along a small mountain stream a half-mile apart in the middle of a beautiful, forested valley. We weren't allowed to have any contact with any of the other eight group members and had to stay within a fifty-yard circle of our personal campsite. Each of us was given crackers, raisins, nuts and three packets of powdered energy drink. I felt bold and desired the challenge of experimenting with a fast so I gave away my food. The first two days I was extremely hungry, but by day three, inspiration surged through me as I felt totally connected to God, Source, The Universe; whatever you wish to call it. I wasn't hungry, felt incredibly creative and sensed an amazing peace wash over me. It was humbling and profoundly powerful. To make my experience even more memorable, I was blessed to go to sleep to the sound of elk bugling nearby.

Sleeping under a simple blue tarp held up by two sticks for twenty-three days made for an interesting sleep. It wasn't quite as secure and convenient as a tent, but it did the job. I used my wool sweatshirt as a pillow and would put my wet boots at the end of my sleeping bag to help dry them out overnight. The quiet solitude, the outline of the distant mountains lit up by an emerging moon and the freedom of being able to pee wherever the heck I wanted under the most beautiful blanket of stars I've ever seen had to be one of the highpoints of my life. Being there helped clear my mind of past failures, future fears and make room for honest dialogue which freed up my intuition and allowed it to guide me to face my challenges with grace. I found myself going inward more than I'd ever been before. I would sit silently and allow thoughts to come up under the sun's warm rays. I began to realize that the only voice I should listen too, was the little voice that spoke from within.

My experience of going into the mountains twenty-five years ago played a crucial role in allowing me learn to trust my intuition and know that it was safe to go inward. Safe and necessary.

Moments of Clarity

What does "go within" mean to you?

How are some ways that you might be able to "go within"?

CHAPTER 45

Have an Open Mind

o·pen

adjective: **open**

1. having no means of closing or barring.
2. completely free from concealment: exposed to general view or knowledge.
   *"She was a very **open**-minded person."*

Legendary writer Mark Twain once shared, "An open mind leaves a chance for someone to drop a worthwhile thought in it." This is something that took me a while to figure out. Not that I thought I had all of the answers, it's just that sometimes I played devil's advocate rather quickly on ideas that were presented to me. Instead of hearing something out, I would immediately begin to express why a particular idea wouldn't work. I used to do that to my dad a lot when we were having discussions about our family business. And I know it drove him nuts. He was a very smart businessman and I was a young "know it all" who didn't know it all. I have come to realize there are a couple of reasons for keeping an open mind and being open to whatever comes your way.

First and foremost is that a different idea might actually be a better way of doing things. You just never know. I can guarantee you that anyone who has ever been successful at anything realizes that he or she does not have all of the answers. And since they realize that they don't have all of the answers, they certainly have had to be open to ideas and suggestions on new ways of doing things along their path to success.

The second reason is that it makes you a better listener. This is a lesson with which most of us can use some help. People appreciate being heard. The more you let other people speak, the more they feel empowered and appreciated. "How does this help me?" you ask. Well, in addition to helping you find possibly some much needed humility; it will also strengthen the bond between you and the person you are connecting with. Whether it's a co-worker, your best friend or a family member, it doesn't matter. It will allow them to feel heard, and that their contributions are important parts of the conversation.

Just remember life moves fast. And because it moves fast, sometimes we are forced to adapt at speeds that aren't always comfortable and we are forced to step out of our comfort zones with ideas. It's ok. Having an open mind is a good thing. You don't always have to say yes to new information or new ways of thinking, but if you are at least open to new ideas it will allow you to live a more fluid, relaxed way of being because you won't be holding on to all that rigid energy that comes with being closed-minded. It is an important part of building your foundation for success.

Moments of Clarity

Are you open to change and hearing other people's ideas?

Do you consider yourself a good listener?

How could you improve your listening skills?

CHAPTER 46

Clear Out and Clean Up

clean

adjective: **clean**

1. free from dirt; unsoiled; unstained.
2. free from foreign or extraneous matter.
   *"He felt much better after moving the boxes and **cleaning** up."*

Do you have things that are just sitting around collecting dust? Is your garage full of stuff that you will never use again? Is your closet full of clothes you will never ever wear? I am guessing your answer is probably yes and if you are anything like me, you feel anxious every time you are reminded of your clutter. The answer is simple, do something about it. Get rid of your unused or unwanted items lying around the house. There are lots of ways to make them disappear. Donate them to a local charity, give them away to friends or sell them.

Stuff has a way of creeping into our lives and before we know it, it starts to take over. Most clutter ends up strangling our energy every time we look at it. Unless you are absolutely going to use an item or finish your project, it is much better to free yourself of the stagnant energy and make room in your life for something new and vibrant. Open up some space in your home. This will allow you to regain your energy and spark your creative juices. The possibilities are endless on what to do with your reclaimed and centered self and renewed wellbeing. Feel the weight lift as you clear out your unwanted items. Having new choices and options is freeing.

Now that you have cleared out your clutter it's time to clean up and make your place shine! How do you feel when you get home from work and notice your house or apartment is dirty or out of sorts? It isn't a nice feeling, is it? It's that same heavy feeling you can get from having too much clutter around. Get rid of that burdensome feeling by tidying up. What might take only a couple of hours will make a huge difference in your attitude and, more importantly, will free up your mind and let you truly relax.

You owe it to yourself. Our homes are where we are supposed to be able to retreat and be at peace. Foundationally speaking our homes are where we springboard forward out into the world and ideally need to be a place where we can let our body, mind and soul rest easy. Clear out and clean up to release the heaviness. I know that I am in a much better flow when my place is cleaned up. I am freed up energetically and feel more optimistic. This simple act always propels me into having a more productive and enjoyable day. I find doing it first thing in the morning is also a great way to get some momentum going. I feel good about the fact that I have accomplished something and I can let that feeling carry me forward. To build and maintain a solid foundation for success, it's quite important that our living space be "livable!"

Moments of Clarity

Do you have any unused items sitting around?

Would your living space be considered clean?

Where are some areas that could be improved?

If these areas were clean, how would that make you feel?

CHAPTER 47

Think Outside the Box

think

verb: **think**

1. to employ one's mind rationally and objectively in evaluating or dealing with a given situation.

2. to have a conscious mind, to some extent of reasoning, remembering experiences.
   "She was able to **think** *mindfully and creatively after meditation."*

I have always been a bit of an outsider and looking back at a lot of my projects, I have to share a bit of a sheepish smile in knowing how I accomplished most of them. I have never been one to really go with the flow. For some reason, I feel like I have to break the rules a bit or go the road less traveled, my own way to be exact, and for the most part it has worked. And if it didn't, at least I gained valuable lessons during the process and knew better the next time.

To think outside the box is to try something new, something out of the ordinary, to take a leap into the unknown and risk falling flat on your face. Boy, did I do all of the above when I set up a workshop and book signing tour back in 2009 for my very first book that I so proudly self-published. My book actually set the process in motion for me to learn how to be a more confident speaker (because it terrified me) and in that same year I began to get my feet wet in the realm of public speaking. I had taken a few community college speech classes, joined a Toastmasters group for a bit, and had just completed putting together an interactive workshop called "An Introduction to Balance" and gave it a test run in front of five of my friends. I really had no idea how it would be received, but was pleasantly surprised when I got a lot of positive feedback. That got me thinking. And while I am not sure where the courage came from, I felt like I was supposed to take the book and workshop on the road. My excitement grew as I got my atlas and started to map out a six-state trip where I would follow a big circle that went from my home at the time, in Reno, Nevada through Utah, Colorado, down to New Mexico, over to Arizona, California, and back up to Reno. I started looking up bookstores and Centers for Spiritual Living that were located in the cities along my route. After making a ton of nervous phone calls, I had a fourteen stop tour lined up and was on the road just three weeks after I gave my friends my workshop test run. I was motivated! My very first stop was in tiny Delta, Utah, a farming community just over the Nevada/Utah border. I did my workshop at their monthly chamber luncheon to a crowd of about nine people. Although I was extremely nervous, they were a kind group of folks and it went pretty well even though they were eating while *interacting* with me. My trip was off and running. While what happened over the course of the next three weeks of the tour is for another time and story, I will say that I was very proud of how I stepped out of my comfort zone, thought out of the box and made my goal happen. There were definitely some things I could have done better. I didn't do a good job of marketing to each of the particular locations prior to arriving. Truth be told, I probably didn't even know how to market my events at the time. I just went for it with unbridled hope, ignorance, and gusto. I will say it was an incredible learning experience for me, even though it wasn't nearly as successful as I hoped. Or maybe I should say it was successful in ways other than selling books and attracting big crowds. I grew a lot through practice, feedback and humility. I will be truthful; it was embarrassing when no one showed up at a few events. It made me question myself. I look back with pride though. It took a lot of guts to put that into motion and make it happen. I had never spoken in public before that trip and I did accomplish my goal. I also learned how to execute even better going forward. What an education I got. I just had to think outside the box a bit to make it happen. And I did. Will I continue to think outside the box going forward? Heck Yes! That's where the gold is.

Moments of Clarity

What does think outside the box mean to you?

How are some ways that you could think outside the box?

CHAPTER 48

Take Care of Your Instrument

in·stru·ment

noun: instrument

1. a tool or implement, especially one used for delicate or precision work.
2. a means whereby something is achieved, performed, or furthered.

   "He cared for his body like it was a fine tuned instrument."

Taking care of ourselves is probably the most important task that we are given yet I don't think enough people give it the importance that it deserves. If your health fails, it can outweigh everything else that's going on in your life. From minor health issues to extremely major ones, poor health can really affect our ability to be happy and live a fulfilling life. I have been blessed with the desire; self-awareness and understanding of the importance of taking care of my body and how it affects the quality of life I live. I want you to live a life of happiness, balance and fulfillment and incorporating the following lifestyle changes into your life will be an incredibly important part of strengthening your foundation toward success.

Drink More Water

Did you know that 60 percent of our bodies and 75 percent of our muscles are made up of water? Is it any wonder that a lot of people get headaches or feel fatigued when they are under hydrated? Did you know that it has been proven that drinking enough water helps many medical conditions? Chronic fatigue, allergies, digestive problems, urinary tract problems and constipation—just to name a few. Did you also know that water acts as a natural appetite suppressant and may help in weight loss? Some other benefits of drinking more water include healthy skin, better nutrient absorption and regulation of body temperature during exercise. I know you've heard this a million times, but if you want your body to feel and operate better, you need to drink more water!

Water not only provides us with invaluable sustenance, it also helps flush out our system; which in turn allows our body to run more efficiently and provide us with more energy. Try having eight glasses of water spread throughout day (eight oz. each). Being properly hydrated is well worth the trouble of having to make a couple of extra pit stops during the day.

I have always been a big water drinker and I know deep down that it is one of the reasons that help me stay in flow and energized. I always keep it at the ready, whether that's in my car, at my desk or by my bedside. Staying hydrated is an important part of my solid foundation!

Moments of Clarity

Are you drinking enough water?

Get More Sleep

According to Thomas Dekker, "sleep is the golden chain that ties health and our bodies together." Are you getting enough sleep? It's an incredibly important part of your foundation. I am at my best when I get 7-8 hours a night. Experiment with this. If you feel like you might need more, allow yourself another hour or two and see if it makes a difference. And please don't think that by taking another hour of sleep each night, out of the 24 hours we have available, that you will be less productive. It has been proven that those who are sleep deficient work more slowly and make more mistakes along the way. Getting more sleep will in turn give you more energy; make you more productive and probably a much happier person. There are many ways to do this; it could be as easy as setting your bedtime earlier and adjusting your schedule, or require some heightened awareness and diligence around your diet. Some people have issues with sleep because of their food choices (sugar, heavy dinners, alcohol, etc.) Sleep deprivation can affect our mood, our concentration, our memory, our ability to fight off infection and our judgment. Inadequate sleep can also lead to weight gain, depression and cause serious health problems such as stroke, heart attack or diabetes.

Sleep is by far the number one catalyst in regard to setting my day up right. If I don't get enough sleep, it's much more difficult to do the other things that help keep me in flow and in balance. Exercise, eating right and meditation for example. When I am sleep deprived, I am not as centered and don't have as much energy to make room for them in my schedule. When I don't keep my routine, I feel quite out of sorts. It affects my confidence, production level, wellbeing and ultimately my ability to be connected to my intuition and others. Not good alternatives. Get more sleep friends. It's worth it.

Moments of Clarity

Are you getting enough sleep? If not, why?

What are some things you could do to allow yourself more sleep?

Go Exercise

Need a little more energy throughout the day? Want to lose a few unwanted pounds? Want to think more clearly and be more productive? Want to feel better about yourself? The answer is simple, go get some exercise.

There are many ways to make exercise a part of your lifestyle, and it's very important to start out at a level that works for you. If you are just beginning, it could be as simple as going for a walk three days a week. The key is to make whatever you do a habit. Not sure where to start? Your local fitness club may be a good place. They typically have a knowledgeable staff available to help you get a program going based on your goals. Don't want to join a gym? No problem. There are many ways to get some exercise that don't require special knowledge or a set of skills you may not have. For example, gardening, swimming (or just splashing around), going to a park and throwing a Frisbee and walking—are just a few. Yoga is also an incredibly valuable way to strengthen your body and mind.

Exercise has always been an important part of my life and has been a major catalyst in helping me build a strong foundation. Team sports, triathlon, hiking and now more recently cross-fit have all helped me build body awareness and confidence that carries over into everything else that I do.

Moments of Clarity

What are some ways that you could get some exercise?

Eat Better Eat Less

How many of you pay attention to how you feel after having a meal or a snack? I hope everyone, but for those that aren't quite there yet, please remember that it's really important to listen to our bodies after we eat. They are definitely talking to us. How might you ask? Primarily through our energy levels. If you are struggling for energy during the day and feel very sluggish after you eat, then you might not be making the best food choices for your body. If you listen to your body it will tell you what works for it and what doesn't. I am not a nutrition expert, but I do know what has worked for me. All those years of training and racing in triathlon helped me become hypersensitive to what I put into my body. And during those years I have learned what food can and cannot do for us. I like to have energy and don't care to feel heavy after a meal so I don't eat too many carbohydrates and extremely limit my sugar/sweets intake. I realize we are all different and what works for me might not work for you, but eating better/eating less has been proven to do so much our bodies, minds and souls. I want you to take away a brand new awareness on what you are eating and how food can affect your mood, production level and ultimately your health.

What is good food? I have always been a fan of moderation, a balance of fruits, vegetables, grains and poultry/ fish/nuts. Basically clean and unprocessed foods. There is so much information out there regarding food studies, food allergies, diets and food lifestyles, (vegetarianism, Keto, veganism, Paleo, just to name a few), that it would be impossible for me to go over it all here. I recommend you go online and do some research to learn more if something piques your interest. There is a wealth of information on healthy eating habits and you will find many sites dedicated to helping people learn about them. I will say that I have experimented with vegetarianism and found that I did better when I added in some poultry and fish. I know that vegetarianism works perfectly well for others. I am not here to tell you what to do, my goal is to help you be more aware of what you are putting into your bodies, so you can then make the best decision for yourself. Do your homework and really see how you feel with your food choices.

Stick to clean food when you can and stay away from food that is processed. Yes, that means most fast food entrees. There is very little nutrition in processed foods and I can guarantee you very little sustainable energy. And please be aware of your sugar intake. It has become known as the "silent killer." Our country is so addicted to sugar that we will do almost anything to continue to satisfy our cravings. I encourage you to look up some articles on how damaging sugar is to our bodies. It will be eye opening to say the least.

Another key to feeling better and more energized is to eat less. We have been trained in this country to super-size everything. Most of us eat way more than we need to during our meals. Try to cut back on your portion sizes. Psychologically it might be hard, but nutritionally I can tell you that you will be just fine. Like any habit, it might take some time, work, and concentration to make the change. But when you do, I promise that you will feel better, have more energy and possibly lose a few pounds. Eating better/eating less is an incredibly important part of keeping your foundation intact and solid.

Moments of Clarity

Do you pay attention to how you feel after you eat a meal?

What are some healthy food choices that you like to eat?

Would you be willing to try other healthy food choices?

What is your current sugar intake?

Meditate

Do you want to feel calmer, carry less stress, have more energy and be more tapped into your intuition? You might want to give meditation a try. Meditation has been life-changing for many people including myself. I am now much more at peace, more relaxed and less anxious than I used to be, since I started this practice about ten years ago. According to Dr. Wayne Dyer, "Meditation is simply the art of being quiet with yourself and shutting down the constant monologue that fills the inner space of your being. And that inner monologue or noise is a shield preventing you from knowing the highest self." In other words, while meditating we are able to give our brain a rest from the busy life and schedule that most of us lead. Which in turn helps us to feel more rested, balanced and centered. And when we are in the space of feeling balanced and rested we are better able to pay attention and listen to our intuition. Intuition is our highest form of intelligence. Why wouldn't we want to tap into that?

There are many forms of meditation and many different ways to meditate. Some people prefer chanting, while others sit silently focusing on their breathing. I recommend doing an Internet search to learn more about the varieties of meditation and what might be best for you. You might want to experiment with a few different styles or take a class and stick with the one that resonates best. I really enjoy going to YouTube and finding guided meditations to listen and relax to. Nothing better than sitting in my favorite chair with a blanket, listening to a soothing meditation refilling my energy cup.

Consistency is very important when starting any meditation program. I realize that you might feel out of your comfort zone while you are getting started, but please stick with it. It will become easier and feel very natural. I enjoy meditating twice a day: once in the morning for about 15 minutes and once before bedtime for the same amount of time.

You may have realized that you are meditating already without even knowing it. Are you into arts and crafts? Do you enjoy painting or drawing? How about gardening or playing a musical instrument? All of these activities can put you into a meditative state. Are you into exercise? Looking back on all of those long training days I put in while I was participating in triathlons, I came to the realization that I would fall into a meditative state while on a long run or a long bicycle ride. I received creative ideas or intuitive thoughts as I moved repetitively for extended periods. Not into running or cycling? You can find the same benefit while going for a walk. Focus on your surroundings and allow yourself to be present and in the moment with what you see. Listening to certain types of music can also help you meditate. I love to listen to ambient music while resting. I also have some favorite instrumentals with meditative beats that I play while writing. It helps me stay in flow, keep my energy up and reach deeper into my intuitive vaults. Meditation is important on so many levels to strengthen your foundation; I encourage you to make it a part of your daily practice. You can start small. Even five minutes a day will help.

I will leave you with the wise words of noted writer and philosopher Ram Dass, "The quieter you become the more you will hear."

Moments of Clarity

How might you incorporate meditation into your life?

Final Thoughts

suc·cess

noun: success

1. a performance or achievement that is marked by success.
2. favorable or measure of succeeding.

   "Anyone who wants to grow and become more self-aware is a **success** *in my book."*

There are many different paths and each one is different. Do not feel that you need to follow another's path. Follow the paths that feel right for you. Create your own habits. Build your own foundation. There are no rules. Cultivate, listen to and trust your intuition, and let it guide your journey. Make it special! Honor what brings you joy, be thankful for all of your gifts and continue to grow.

All of your learning experiences up to this point have made you who you are and have set the stage for the rest of your wonderful life. Be proud of YOU, what you have to work with and strive to be your best.

Greatness is already within all of us. Sometimes we just need to peel away a few layers and do some inner housework to access it. I invite you to look within, to be open to new ideas and practice new habits from what I have shared with you. It is my sincere hope that you can learn, grow, and solidify your own foundation to be the best version of yourself. I believe in you and I want you to believe in yourself. I encourage you to remember to laugh along the way, pick yourself up when you fall down, and know that it's a journey, not a destination. The path will change, you will change, it might look different than when you started and that's all okay. I'm still making discoveries every day as I follow my own path. My practices and my habits have helped me to build a strong foundation and from there, I believe anything is possible.

Your Voice

Your voice creates a ripple
Over land and well beyond
Truthful words vibrate lifted
To create a loving bond

Your voice can be your freedom
Or your voice can be your hell
Mindful heed in word and thought
Send forth love and light to gel

Your voice can give permission
To another seeking truth
Authentic, centered living
Tap's into eternal youth

Your voice can be the difference
To set a young child free
Loving words to encourage
A model for them to be

Your voice is your ready key
To unlock your truthful worth
Spoken pure, life now renewed
Energized, loving, rebirth

Your voice gives inspiration
For those afraid to speak
Reassuring tones shared true
Helps others gain their peak

Your voice is a kindred link
When spoken face to face
True connection eyes unite
Before texting took its place

Your voice is your true freedom
When it's spoken from the heart
Intuition's guiding path
Helps you play your destined part

Your voice is fundamental
For all life and love to flow
Empowered, valued, perfect
Painting a worldly glow

—G. Brian Benson

Acknowledgments

To the reader, thank you for joining me on this journey. I hope this book will help inspire you on yours.

Special thanks to my family—I appreciate and love each and every one of you. Thank you for the love, the support, the laughs and the lessons. To my son Michael, I couldn't be more proud of who you are and who you are becoming.

To my amazing friends and acquaintances near and far, I wish I could list you all. Just know that you are all in my heart and very much appreciated. Thank you for the friendship and love!

My dear friend Susannah Rose Woods a.k.a. "Twin." You are an amazing writer and were an invaluable content editor for me on this project. Thank you for the friendship. You are loved and appreciated.

They say every coach needs a coach, and Lisa Solterbeck has been that for me. Thank you, dear friend, for the guidance, love and friendship through the years.

My friend and agent Kristin Moeller of Waterside Literary Agency, thank you for helping make a dream of mine come true.

To all of the wonderful people who have believed in me, offered help, grown with me, presented an opportunity or collaborated on a project. Sincere thanks.

And thank you to Brenda Knight and everyone at Mango Publishing for giving me this opportunity. Let's have some fun and make a difference!

Bibliography and Resources

Chapter 3: Strive For Balance—Coach Training Alliance. "Strive for Balance" works inspired by Coach Training Alliance, LLC., Coach Training Manual. *2003–2005.*

Chapter 6: It's OK to Fail—G. Brian Benson. "A Minute of Failure." *2008*

Chapter 9: Be Vulnerable—G. Brian Benson. "Light." *2011*

Chapter 13: Just Be You—G. Brian Benson. "Come On Down." *2013*

Chapter 17: Have Patience While Learning—G. Brian Benson. "We Are Meant to Succeed." *2008*

Chapter 23: Clean Up Your Disagreements—G. Brian Benson. Stanza from "Keys to Life." *2009*

Chapter 26: Go Play—G. Brian Benson. "Play." *2012*

Chapter 27: Create Awareness—Mukesh Mani. "A Man and His Horse." Published Sept. 28, 2017—http://www.outofstress.com/self-realization-short-stories/

Chapter 35: Be Easy on Yourself—G. Brian Benson. Stanza from "Keys to Life." *2009*

Chapter 38: Allow Yourself to Feel—G. Brian Benson. "Awake." *2012*

Chapter 49: Final Thoughts—G. Brian Benson. "Your Voice." *2012*

To learn more about Brian, his coaching, podcast, past and future projects, TEDx presentation, as well as to sign up for his newsletter please go to:

www.gbrianbenson.com

You can follow Brian at:

Twitter—@gbrianbenson

Instagram—@gbrianbenson

Facebook—@gbrianbensonmedia

YouTube—@gbrianbenson

About the Author

G. Brian Benson's mission is to wake up the world with conscious, thought-provoking media that inspires. In 2008, Brian followed a hunch and left his family's business, stepping into the unknown. Ever since, inspiration has followed. Letting intuition be his guide, he began to step out of his comfort zone and unexpected paths and talents started to emerge such as writing, acting, and crafting stories. Tapping into this emerging creativity, Brian began his own hero's journey of self-realization and growth, which continues to influence his empowering and inspiring books, films, and presentations.

Brian is an award-winning and #1 bestselling author, coach, radio personality, actor, filmmaker, creative, and TEDx speaker, who knows the value of trusting intuition and wants to share his own personal journey of self-growth, discovery, and accomplishment to help others reconnect with their own personal truths to live an authentic and fulfilling life. As a four-time Ironman triathlete and cross-country bicyclist, Brian knows the value of hard work and never giving up on his dreams, a message he shares with audiences through each of his creative expressions.

Brian currently lives in Los Angeles, CA.

9 781633 538665